GW01605512

First edition published
Published by: The Foundation For Transpersonal Consciousness

British Library Cataloguing in Publication Data

A catalogue record of this book is available from the British library

ISBN 978-0-9568403-1-8

HOW THE BANKS ARE SCREWING YOU

&

WHAT YOU CAN DO ABOUT IT

Index

Contents:

Acknowledgments

Over the few short months working on these pages, I have been supported by many people whom I have had the privilege of meeting, as well as those I have yet to meet in person. Each have been wonderful in their encouragement, as well as sharing their thoughts, feelings and understanding of what is happening in relation to the world of finance that in recent years has gone totally mad, and having now arrived at a place of seemingly unrecoverable insanity. Those I wish to recognise, though not by name, as they number into the high hundreds, include an array of Irish people whom I encountered while hosting and facilitating weekly support meetings for those experiencing financial difficulties. Thank you for being there, for sharing your voice and your stories. Most of all, thank you for having the courage to stand up to the system.

Thank you Paola, Gerry, Gabriel, Michael, Liz, Mary and Teresa for your valued feedback, and thanks also to those who have inspired me through their writings in this area and related fields. It was from your vision that I have found a likeness that encourages me to say 'what the heck, let's shout it out'; Mary Elizabeth Croft, Vince Khan, Tom Schauf and Chris Field to name but a few. Throughout this book I have attempted to keep all the work and wording my own, although I took inspiration from an aspect of Tom Schauf's writings and used a small number of the fantastically worded questions that ask what I was asking only in a more powerful way. Thanks Tom for your work, experience and vision.

If anyone believes that their work is referenced here without due credit, please forgive the oversight. The intention was to write in my own style and not to use anyone's work, but only share what I had discovered. In truth, the information in a book of this nature belongs to all of us, and its contents should be offered for use and reference to everyone.

Thank you to all within Bank of Ireland, Permanent TSB Bank, Ulster Bank and Allied Irish Bank who spoke off the record. I appreciate your confirmation that the information in this book is correct. I am sorry that you are working in a world that causes you to be afraid of the things we discussed, but as you explained, you are protecting your jobs and your families. I hope you soon see that there is life beyond the system. Furthermore, thank you to the legal people who advised me to check into rehab or residential facility for 'loppers'. Many of you affirmed that I was not only right in what I am saying in this book but utterly mad to say it... I will not be checking in the suggested loony bin and you can rest assured that the freedom of the people of Ireland will certainly not be a result of your enthusiasm for self empowerment. Finally, to the Judge who 'off the record' told me that I was not 'free' and that he would hold me in contempt if I ever turned up in his court and challenged him with some of my wild thoughts and my questionable personality, thank you for making me laugh so much...

In advance, thank you all for buying this book, now spread the great news and let us create a new experience of life together.....without the B.S.

Finally and with all my heart, thank you Paola. You are my rock, angle and guide. You are my joy, my warrior and hope. You are my laughter, healer, breath, loyal truth and my incredible wife whom I love with all I have. Gaia is proud of you and all you do for her.... me too x

Introduction

Writing about the banks, the legal system and the financial struggles of the people of Ireland was never on my radar as a 'must do', nor was it a 'need to' or a 'might do', rather I found myself in a situation over the last few years where clients were experiencing overwhelming levels of desperation, fear and anxiety as a result of the current economic situation and I was simply compelled to do something. I heard the same stories from different people about the banks and the court system, which had resulted in the powerlessness that many were feeling as they watched everything they had worked for being taken away. I listened to people who were considering suicide, heard from others who had attempted it and was moved by the stories of those who had succeeded in ending their own life. Sitting with people who spoke through so many tears was truly challenging and knowing that things could be different, knowing that people didn't need to feel so lost and broken but saying little as I listened was the greatest challenge of all. To see such exhaustion and resignation was heart breaking when there is never any need to feel that suicide, depression, medication or running away is the only option.

In response to the relentless call for someone to do something I began to hold support meetings which informed people of the true nature of the banking crises and how they were caught up in a financial and legal game. Every week the hotel room would be full of men and women who had travelled from all over Ireland to sit for a few hours in the hope of being heard and supported. Many could no longer find the objectivity that would allow them a different perspective on things, so that they could break free from the mental, emotional and physical torture that was consuming them.

In an attempt to help those present I would speak of my own understanding of life and belief in our power to challenge the oppression and madness of what is labelled as 'normal' and 'society'. During the following months I explained how the illusions around us have a powerful effect on who we think we are and what we assume is the meaning and purpose of life. I talked about how we live in a world guided by beliefs and facts that once examined often turn out to be not so factual at all.

In the following pages, I will elaborate on how my own questioning has led me to a place of understanding how our reality is created, including the banking and legal reality. For those who choose to question there is a significant awakening in store. This is because life is not necessarily what it seems, and through the questioning process you will understand that you have a choice in how you can see and experience life, at which point you can begin to create your own experience of the life you want to live.

The banking world has taken much from the people of Ireland, and will continue to do so until WE realise that we have the power, the freedom and strength to change that. The power of the bank is only as great as your fear of it. The governments, past and present have continually lied to you, turned their back on you and sold your freedom so that they can look good on the European stage, feel good around their great banqueting tables and tell each other how the country would be screwed if it was not for them. Well, the country is screwed because *of* them, but you are not screwed, and depending on your perception of life, your entire reality can be changed from one of struggle to freedom and joy. All you need to do is to step forward and claim your life, your independence and freedom. The question is simple, 'have you had enough'? Until the answer is a resounding 'yes' you will continue to allow the abuse, lies, cheating and deceit to continue. However, if you decide to change, you will see that you are not just a number nor are you a fool who deserves to be left ignorant. You do not need to be afraid to tear up the rulebook if the rules are preventing you and your children from enjoying a peaceful and happy future.

My intention is that by the end of this book you will understand that the money game is an illusion, that you do not owe the bank any money and that the legal system is not here to help you. Furthermore, the government has no idea of who you are, what you need or how to grasp the true nature of what troubles you.

As you read, I urge you to do so with a heart and mind that are focused on what is possible. If frustration or bitterness is triggered just stay focused on what can be done. There is just cause to be angry as the systems that were meant to protect you have left you confused and powerless. Certainly feel these feelings and then replace them with knowing that you can change the reality of life from what it is today to what it can be tomorrow.

It is time for revolution, but the change I speak of needs no guns, violence, bloodshed or hatred. It is a revolution of consciousness and the beginning of an awakening which will result in the reclaiming of our power, rights, freedom and the voice that has been silenced by those who have forgotten their place and what matters most.

We are a free people, let us act accordingly. We are a powerful people, let us live from that power. We are a creative people, let us create. We are a heart centred people, let us agree to make the changes we need from love and give ourselves and those who come after us a reason to smile. We are the ancestors of the future. What is the legacy we wish to leave to our people?

Open your eyes, educate your mind, think critically, look within and see the magic that is there. Let us reclaim our power, together.

As a final note: as you read through the content of this book you will come across some pretty stark generalisations and criticisms of the people who work within the different systems, in particular the banks and the legal system. I am very well aware that most people are well intended and good natured, I am confident that most people would not aim to hurt anyone else. I would ask that you read those elements of the book with an understanding that there are exceptions to every rule and not everyone in the system is out to get, hurt or upset other people. That being said I am not apologising for the stark generalisations made as I am highlighting the significant and real issues that exist in our society. If you are one of the people within the system that takes offence to what is said in this book as you are simply trying to do an honest day's work for an honest day's pay I apologise to you personally, I am not referring to you, I am talking about the idiot down the corridor from you, you know who I mean.

HOW THE BANKS ARE SCREWING YOU

&

WHAT YOU CAN DO ABOUT IT

Chapter 1

The Earth Is Not Flat

Did You Know

- Many people in Ireland are falling into depression, experiencing extreme stress and considering, attempting or succeeding in committing suicide because of financial pressure.
- Educating yourself about how the financial and legal system work can free you from debt.
- Even though its sounds unbelievable you do not actually owe the banks any money.

All names in the following three stories have been changed.

Mary: A True Story

Married with three children, Mary dreamed of working for herself. She had spent her life doing what she needed to ensure that her children would be provided for, her husband could rest when he arrived home from work and as a family they could spend quality time together on holidays. She wanted family dinners and romantic Christmases that were filled with the kind of gifts that her own family could not afford when she was younger.

Mary worked in the property rental business for eleven years, often putting in an eighteen hour day. After sending the children to school, she would leave for work, and once a week she and her husband would meet for lunch. Finally, after many years Mary saw the chance to improve her life by going into the property business with a colleague. It was not long before they had a strong rental business and a deposit on two apartments in the city which they had acquired by releasing equity on their respective family homes.

By 2006 Mary owned many apartments and never missed a bank payment. Her family had their dream holiday and the last number of Christmases had been a wonderful experience for everyone.

Two years later in November 2008 things began to change when the bank called in the €80,000 overdraft. Using the spending capital that was to support the business, Mary and her partner managed to pay half the amount but with nothing left, things were going to be more difficult.

By August 2009 Mary's rental income is less than her monthly repayments. She is also losing tenants and others are no longer able to pay the agreed amount. Mary now owes the bank €1.8 million, and her monthly income is equal to 20% of what is due out. She pays the bank what she can but it is never enough. The banks are now saying that they want full payment on the loans.

By May 2010, the bank has called in almost €1 million of the debt. Mary feels distracted most of the time and her children are not getting her attention. Coupled with this, she cannot afford the €18,000 cash upfront payment that her legal council are demanding to represent her. Mary's husband has also lost his job.

By July 2011 Mary has lost most of her property and family income. Her health and marriage are also suffering. In addition, the family home mortgage has not being paid for almost eight months. Mary is going to counselling but is lost in the fear of what happens next. She feels responsible for the entire situation and has stopped opening mail, and avoids bank phone calls.

By October 2011 Mary feels that her marriage is over. If she were to pay off all her bank debt and take care of the judgments that are against her it would take her almost 25 years with monthly payments of over €7,000. She is due in court again in a couple of months as the bank is now after her family home. Any rental income she had from remaining investments is gone since the bank took over the business via their receivers. Mary is now on anti-depressants. The bank has told her that she can always phone the Samaritans. Whether you see it or not, Mary is your sister and she is hoping that someone will do something that will make a difference.

Richard: A True Story

R.I.P. Although Richard spent his life working hard he ended up in debt to the bank for €3.2 million. Over the years he had often borrowed for his business but had repaid everything on time and without challenge. In spite of which, he would comment to his family that the only worry was knowing that he owed the bank a 'few bob', and when they refused to restructure his loans and closed off all lines of support his life became very difficult. They also informed him that if he did not make the payments that he would lose everything within the year. The bank's attempt to pressure Richard to resolve the issue hit him hard and gave life into his greatest worry - not being able to repay his debt.

Richard was found hanging from the neck with bailing twine. His family have told me that their only wish now is that his sixteen year old son will learn to deal with the memory of finding him and not being able to cut him down. It seems that the memory of trying to lift his father to create slack and then discovering that he could not reach the rope to cut it has had the greatest impact on him.

The bank official has said that they will only deal with a solicitor or an intermediary in trying to find a way for the family to honour the debt they inherited with the estate as the family are too emotional to deal with them directly. Richard's family are beautiful people and he was a great father.

Mark: A True Story

Mark had little debt compared to his peers in their early thirties. He had borrowed €330,000 for a house, owed €12,000 on two credit cards and had an overdraft of €3,000 as well as a personal loan of €14,000 and a car finance loan.

Mark earned almost €65,000 per annum which easily covered his monthly repayments. However, he lost his job, and by January 2011 his savings were being used to service his debt repayments. Eventually Mark could only afford to pay the bank a small amount each month from his welfare payments, which did not even cover the interest. Mark is now in arrears with his mortgage and his other debts are worth more than they were at the beginning of the year. The bank has repossessed his car and they are still chasing him for the loan. He is trying to find a job but believes that he will have to emigrate in the coming months. He wants to know 'what the F*** just happened'.

I, and many of my family, neighbours and friends have been getting demand letters from the banks in relation to loans and mortgages that are starting to fall into arrears. We do not know what to do or where this will end. What do I need to do?

There is a way through this and you can be confident in knowing that you have the power to do what is needed in order to structure your life into a balanced, measured and positive experience.

Here is what I am hearing from most of the people I speak with in relation to bank debt.

- They have monthly payments to make to the bank that are higher than the money coming in.
- The payments are often interest only and in many cases these people cannot afford to pay all the interest, which means that people are giving the bank all they have, even though this does not change the amount owed. In fact, often the debt and the outstanding balance continue to rise.
- Even if people work for the next twenty years and pay the bank all they can, the debt will remain. Meanwhile their quality of life has been lost.
- Many people now know that their property is so low in value that even if they did manage to pay it off, they will have paid far in excess of its selling value, and they are starting to wonder if they should bother.
- Many people are starting to experience anxiety, stress, broken relationships, heart attacks, strokes, suicides and depression.
- Many people are realising that they need to change their perspective in order to move through this mess.
- Many people are feeling the need to prioritise their health and life and to gain the confidence to tell the bank where to go.

What can we do?

1. Educate yourself about the financial system and how it works.
2. Educate yourself about the legal system and how it works.
3. Educate yourself about the true nature of who you are, why you are here and what your life is about.
4. Take a stand with your new knowledge and change the experience of life that you are having, because in doing so you will change the situation you find yourself in with the banks and with every other aspect of your life.

What are you implying when you say 'educate yourself' in relation to these things?

Knowledge gives you the ability to empower or disempower others. Depending on your intention you will either free the world and the people around or you will imprison them. Knowledge puts you on the road that leads to wisdom, courage, confidence, action and ultimately freedom. To live without educating yourself is to choose a life where you can never know what to do. Right now, things are as they are because people have been misled, lied to and manipulated. Those with the knowledge have been keeping everybody else blind, numb and ignorant. So the most powerful thing you can do is to educate yourself because what you will discover will change your beliefs which will then change your world.

What will I discover if I begin to educate myself in these things?

You will discover that many of the beliefs you were raised to accept as true are in fact untrue. You will also learn that you have been programmed into a way of thinking that allows the 'game of life' to continue, at a significant cost to you.

What will I learn about the banks and the current situation we are in?

You will discover that the banking system is a business built on illusions and designed to keep you paying vast sums of money in order to keep it wealthy and you poor. As we continue in the conversation you will discover that:

1. You do not owe the bank any money for mortgages, loans or other alleged financial debt.
2. The government, banks, legal system, education system, the church system and the health system are all managed by a certain kind of 'mindset' and until that is changed you will continue to remain ignorant and poor and they will continue to control of your life.
3. You will discover that the banks are managing the greatest con job ever by creating a world that depends on money, and facilitates them as the keepers of that money when the world would be better off if we created a new understanding of wealth.

What do you mean that I do not owe any money for my mortgage?

1. You do not owe money for your mortgage, because the nature of money makes it impossible to owe anything.
2. You do not owe anything to the bank because you never borrowed from them. You were simply led to believe that you did.

You now have the power to stand up and say 'no' to the system that is pushing you over the cliff of anxiety, fear, depression and poverty. No matter what you are told is right or wrong you can take back control of your life, it is you that creates reality. Even if you do not know you are doing so you are always creating your reality.

'stand up and say 'no' to the system that is pushing you over the cliff'

In the next chapters you will be required to suspend your way of thinking in order to understand the amazing lie you have been living and the astonishing amount of denial that exists in the world in order for it to continue as it is. The following few points are true but if you do not suspend your current beliefs you will be blinded by the impression they create.

- You do not owe the bank any money.
- You have been lied to and misled for the most of your life.
- You did not create the current economic crisis and you do not have to pay for it to be balanced out.

- The rules of life written by the Government can be changed, deleted, used to light the fire or ignored. You are sovereign being who has the power to change the world.

Take a deep breath and see that things are not as they seem.

Chapter 2

The Illusion of Money

Did You Know

- Money is made out of thin air and has no true value.
- You have been misled, lied to and manipulated by the banks into thinking that you took a loan when you did not.
- You were never meant to understand the money game, nor were you meant to realise your true power.

Where has all the money gone?

It has gone nowhere because it never existed. We were told that the global economy had gone through a surge, and finally after many generations of getting it wrong we had cracked the code that unlocked the hidden wisdom of wealth, abundance and the endless supplies of all that we needed to be happy.

We wanted to believe that a balance had been created that would allow the flow of money in such a way that we could buy everything we were told would make us happy. But the wealth with which we were buying properties, travelling the world and watching grow in our accounts was an illusion. It never existed. You were just lead to believe that it did.

Imagine a small child who is convinced that there is a bogyman in the wardrobe. The belief in the bogyman has such a powerful effect that her entire life becomes a living breathing experience of someone who is about to be taken away by this monster, never to be seen again. Her vitals all change to correspond with that belief. In fear of what happens next her blood pressure increases, her breathing becomes heavy and fast and her hands sweat. Finally, her voice will echo at such a pitch that anyone within ear shot will come running. Her belief that the bogeyman is there is her reality and in that moment the bogeyman exists.

Why did the child believe the bogeyman was there in the first place?

Because of the environment she lives in, the culture of the world of television, children's story books and the traditional, misunderstood teaching of life that gets passed down through the generations.

What has this got to do with money and bank debt?
A lot, and not just money and bank debt. It speaks to us about all of life and the pillars we believe hold it all together; money/banks, god/religions, medicine/health and hospital service, politics/governments, fairness/legal systems... but let us stay focused on the money bit for now.

The first hurdle to jump is the belief that money is an illusion for the same reason as our young friend may find it hard to believe that the bogeyman also is an illusion. After all, how can something that makes your heart beat faster, your hands sweat, your voice squeak and your blood boil not be real?

Are you saying that money is not real?
Money is real and at the same time it is not real. The money in your pocket is real but most of the money 'in' the bank is not. Only 3% of all money in circulation is in cash, the other 97% are figures on a computer screen with no cash in the vault to back them up. All this is a matter of perception; in fact life is experienced as a result of perception and nothing more. If you think outside the norm you will realise that the 'money' concept is a game and money has no real or true place, value or worth. We have simply been brainwashed into believing that money

is what the authorities tell us it is and without it we cannot manage. These are lies and untruths. Money is an illusion and with this realisation we can eliminate much that is wrong with society such as theft, greed, robbery, hunger, homelessness and depression.

How can money be an illusion when I bought my house with it, shop with it, get paid my salary with it, give it to the tax man and he leaves me alone (for now)? How can money not be real when it is the centre piece of life and everything revolves around it?

Imagine everyone wants to withdraw their savings at the same time. It would not take long before the bank shut its door and put the sign, 'no money left'. This is because there is insufficient money in the vault to honour the savings. It does exist and it never did.

'Sorry, No Money Left'

Think about it. If the population of the country has a combined wealth of €1000 according to their bank statements, and when they try to withdraw it the banks close their doors and declares there is no money left after only €100 has been withdrawn, this tells us that the money does not exist. Someone has created an illusion to make us believe that money exists when it does not. In this case, that the world believes it has €900 more than it actually has.

But money does exist, even if it is less than what we thought?
Go back to the little girl and the bogeyman.

There is no bogeyman!!! It is an illusion!

…but you can be sure that when Daddy tells her that it is an illusion she will fight to prove that the bogeyman exists. The answer is that the few notes you see being withdrawn only make you think that there is money. You will soon realise that not only is money an illusion but there is much about your life that will change once you shift your perception. A new perception could even create a money free world where you have everything you need without the challenges to attain it. The good news is that your future can be different if you allow yourself to see through the illusion and understand the difference between what is and what is not real.

How could we spend the money if it never existed?
Because it suits the system(s) for you to believe that the money game is not a game, because then you assume that without money you could not have your home, car, fuel, groceries, holidays and new clothes.

But on Thursday I got my salary and on Friday I paid the electricity?

Did you really get money (cash) on Thursday and pay for the electricity from this cash or did your employer give you a pay slip and lodge it into your account? It is more likely that your employer gave someone instructions to transfer numbers from a computer into an account in your name and you paid the electricity with a cheque or another electronic transfer.

Regardless of what happened you did not get money, you got 'credit' on a screen and then transferred a percentage of that credit to a third party. The reality remains that if we all go to the bank to take out our money it will not be there because money does not exist. You are playing the game with the illusion of money and not the money that you can hold in your hands.

So if I didn't pay with money, why hasn't the electricity company come looking for me?

Because they are playing the game too! You see, if money does exist, why is the world's economy experiencing the worst meltdown in history? Does it not strike you as odd that there once was a lot of money and now there is none? How can something that is real not be real? Maybe it was never real to begin with.

Why is the system creating this illusion?

The most valuable thing that the illusion gives the few who manage it is the power to create what they want, when they want and for whatever reason they want, and you are just a pawn in their game of creating life according to their agenda. If we believed that money opens the door to riches and happiness then we would all be in the rat race making as much money as possible. However, the purpose of the illusion of money is not to give money a value but to make us think that it has value, so that you can buy what you need and invest in what you want in order to create more of the illusion. Whereas all this does is allow for a transfer of the wealth, albeit an illusion. This illusion of new money and wealth that is created is continually travelling back into the hands of the few that are running the show.

When the collective population become too wealthy they are put back in their box via recessions

Look at this from another perspective, let's say that the illusion of money is created and we accept it as real and all of a sudden we waken up to realise that all the money is now in the hands of a small number of people. What does this translate into? It translates into the realisation that these few people control all the wealth and everything that the wealth can be used for. This gives them incredible power and control over the lives of everyone who believes in the wealth and accepts that it is in the hands of a few. As long as we believe it to be, it will be.

So, if 'money' isn't real, what is the true currency?
Perception is the true currency. Your perception is based on your beliefs which, in turn create the horizon you look upon. Perhaps it is now time for each of us to change our perception and begin to see life from a different angle. Once we do this, be assured that everything will change.

Chapter 3

You Do Not Owe Anything

Did You Know

- The banks have most likely sold off all your 'alleged' debt.
- The true nature of money is debt and the true nature of debt is such that it can never be cleared.
- The banks need you to be in debt in order to make money. The main purpose of the bank is to make a profit and for that to happen they must ensure that you are not released from your debt.

The 'money is an illusion' concept makes sense, I see that all around me. But what if you are wrong?

I am not, but I can see that you need reassurance. Let us say that the bank did give you a loan of their actual money from their vault, you still owe nothing.

Why?

There are a number of reasons why you don't owe anything at all. Let's start with the most obvious. Assuming the banks did give you their money you no longer owe them anything because they were bailed out and once they received that money your debt was cleared because their big hole of nothingness was filled in with the bailout fund and the collective taxes of the population are effectively what is being used to settle that bill. So your taxes are paying off the debt that was used to pay off all the debt.

Give me another reason why I do not owe anything?

You do not owe them anything because money has no true value and you cannot owe anything for something that has no value.

What does that mean?

Money is a liability and it does not have a true value, especially in the commonwealth countries that have no gold or silver backing or supporting it. Once upon a time money was backed by precious metals and it was possible to exchange notes for gold or silver, and it was this promise to exchange your note (money) for a precious metal that gave it its value. But there no longer exists enough precious metal for this promise to be upheld, nor does the government hold any precious metals to support the notes in circulation and therefore it is tradable for nothing other than what our collective confidence agrees it is tradable for. The money is only worth what we agree among ourselves that it is worth, which is determined by what we say we are willing to trade for it.

What do you mean by 'money is always a liability'?

Many people believe that money is worth something when the creation of money is only the creation of debt. Once a euro note falls off the end of the conveyor belt it is sold into the banking system. The price it fetches is the face value plus an interest rate.

So, if €50 is sold at a rate of one percent to the banking world that €50 starts its life in a negative figure and the one per cent owed on it is its true value. This means that the €50 is actually representative of €50.50 debt. Furthermore, say one million euro is created. Most of us believe that the world is now one million euro better off, whereas what has really happened is that debt has been created to the value of one percent of one million euro, plus the one million itself. In order to settle the debt we must pay one million plus one percent. How can this be done if only the one million exists and the one per cent does not? It cannot be done and therefore the world continues to print money in order to pay debt, but in printing it, it is actually creating debt. The illusion continues and the wealth keeps going to the same people all the time.

Take a moment to think this through... all the money in the world represents a debt i.e. the percentage above its face value plus the perceived value of the money itself. So in order to create a situation where we settle the world's debt, we need to create more money in order to have the percentage above the face value of all the money, but that will not clear the debt because the creation of the extra money simply creates more debt. So, money is debt and nothing more. Therefore the debt is represented by money that does not exist so we can say that both money and debt are illusions, and we are the greatest players in the game of keeping it alive.

So what if we just created money and distributed it as interest free?

This is a key idea for creating a better future that right now the banks, government, politicians or legal system do not want, as it would kill their wealth, or the illusion of their wealth, and they would lose their control.

So I do not owe money because the bank has been bailed out and because money has no value and you cannot owe something that is a nothing and I do not owe money because money is debt. Are there any other reasons why I do not owe money?

Apart from all the reasons given so far, you do not owe the bank any money for your mortgage because they sold your debt in their securitization process.

What does that mean?

It means that they have sold your debt to a third party. In the securitization process the banks sold off parts of their asset book to other banks, financial institutions, pension funds, investment brokers, corporations and anyone else who came along and showed a buying interest. The whole securitization business was based on the fractional reserve banking model which I will explain later and effectively the bank turned your signature into a promissory note and sold it on the open market. When they sold your debt it was then cleared. It is possibly now owned by Mr Wong in China or Mr Goldman in the USA or Ms Somebody in Canada or by a lot of different organisations around the world.

Here is a story that will help you understand the concept of not owing anything on the back of the bank selling your debt; Paul lends Mark ten euro and, after months of trying to get repaid his ten euro, Paul gets frustrated at Mark's refusal to pay it back. Eventually James says to Paul that he will buy the debt for eight euro. Of course Paul is starting to think that he will never get a penny back so he accepts the eight euro and knows that Mark now owes him nothing. James then knocks on Marks front door and once Mark answers James says 'you owe me ten euro'. Upon hearing this Mark says "who are you? What makes you think I owe you anything? I don't know you, I have never met you and I certainly have never agreed any business with you nor have I given anybody my permission to do business with you on by behalf. Sling your hook and don't come back." Who would blame Mark for reacting in such a manner? Someone cannot simply sell your debt and leave you in a relationship with another party without your being a part of the discussions that led to that actuality.

What do I say to the bank when they say I do own them money for my mortgage?

You ask them to prove to you beyond all doubt that they are the legal party of interest in the case.

What does that mean?

Effectively the bank is saying that you owe them money and you are asking them to prove it. For in order for the bank to make you repay your 'debt' they must prove that you owe it.

You are now aware that the bank has sold your mortgage to another party and this means that they have 'no legal standing in the case' against you. They are now a collection agent on behalf of another party but they are not the true party of interest and for this reason they have no legal grounds to take you to court. This is because someone else owns the debt and the chances are that they cannot even identify the true owner of the debt as the securitization process has split the debt into so many pieces that it no longer exists in its original form.

Let us say that one hundred people buy one orange each and the one hundred people sell their oranges to ten orange dealers at a small profit. Some of the ten orange dealers then sell on the oranges to a number of orange juice companies at a profit and the rest sell their oranges onto other organisations that believe that they can use the oranges for their businesses. The orange juice people then squeeze all the oranges into juice and sell the juice by the cup to a lot of different people and all the time each transaction making a small profit.

> ***'You cannot get oranges from orange juice'***

For whatever reason a few of the original orange owners decide that they are not happy with all the money that was made on the sale of what was their orange and they feel hard done by so they call the people in the juice company and say they want their orange back. What happens now? Well, you cannot get oranges from orange juice. This is the way it is with your mortgage. It has been split up, sold on, split up again and sold on again and this has happened so many times that the original mortgage no longer exists. How can you be held responsible to pay on something that does not exist and cannot be proven? The reality is that your bank is not the true party of interest and they have no legal standing in the case.

If you watch what is happening in the USA at the moment you will see that many people who lost their homes in the last five years through repossession are now being handed back their homes. In some states the courts are even ruling that many, if not all, foreclosures since 2008 are void for the reasons outlined to you here. The States of Massachusetts and Kansas are two that have made significant rulings in relation to this.

But I took out a mortgage, didn't I?

Did you? If you say you did you did. But you have to ask some serious questions about what you believed you were entering into at the time and what you believe you are engaged in now. Go back to the bogeyman in the wardrobe, the little girl can feel all the feelings and experience all the experiences that confirm there is a bogeyman there. If you were to sit with her and ask her you might even find that she saw and heard something in the wardrobe that further

'you have to ask some serious questions about what you believed you were entering into at the time and what you believe you are engaged in now'

confirmed her fear that the bogeyman was real and was there. In that moment, considering her belief and the level of emotional, psychological and physical investment in the experience she is having, the bogeyman is there in her world but to Daddy the bogeyman is not there. So the bogeyman is there and he is not there. The question is what perspective you choose to consider this from. Just because something seems real it does not mean that it is real but neither does it mean that you cannot have an experience as if it is real.

Right now I don't know what to do. All I know is that something is wrong, something doesn't feel right and I know that I am being unfairly treated just so the bankers and the other people behind them can have what they want. I cannot understand what this has all been about. What has the last 20 years of my life been for?

It seems that you are stuck between old beliefs and new beliefs, and the confusion arises from the knowledge that there is still more to know, more pieces of the jigsaw puzzle to find.

I do believe that you are now beginning to realise that there is an aspect to all of this that needs to be tapped into and considered in order to fully understand what is real and what is not. I cannot encourage you enough in relation to exploring that - it is in the exploration of the bigger picture that you will find all the sense and meaning you are looking for.

So, I shouldn't worry too much about being in arrears then?

It is not that simple unfortunately but to be truly honest NO, you shouldn't worry too much about it. I would however strongly suggest that you learn the ins and outs of what we are talking about as the legal system that is attached to the financial system may not see it this way without some serious persuasion, but we will chat about that later on also. I will say this however, if you are in arrears for more than twelve months it is very possible that your loan has been cleared at a provision figure with an internal banking default insurance policy. And not only that, the bank will have received a tax write off on the 'bad debt'.

Sum it up for me.

The bank was paid for this loan by a bailout fund. They also sold this debt on the open market and made money there from it as well as benefiting from a default insurance policy. On top of that received a tax right off for the debt and are still coming after you to pay them what you do not owe. Remember we are talking about the reality of you not owing the bank anything in the context of 'money being real and holding a true value' but we know that money is only an illusion.

It makes me mad just thinking about it?

Do not get mad, just get happy knowing that you are starting to see through the illusion and spend some time learning how to change your reality.

Is it possible to change my reality and have a different experience of life other than this one?

Absolutely YES! There is a way out of this mess but it begins with accepting that the money reality is only an illusion. I am happy to chat with you about what you can do in a little while but there is some more information worth having first.

Chapter 4

Your Signature Creates Money

Did You Know

- You created the money that the bank 'allegedly' loaned you.
- The bank lied to you when they told you that they gave you their money.
- You funded the capital that the banks used to fund your alleged loan.

We just discussed that I don't owe the bank any money in the context of money having a true value. So, what about money being 'an illusion'? Explain how that works in the context of not owing the bank anything.

You do not owe anything to the banks for your mortgage, loans, overdrafts, car finance or credit cards. Let me explain. In recent years I sat with a senior manager in one of Ireland's main banks and explained to him that I was aware of the fact that once a mortgage (or other loan) was agreed it was lodged into the bank's asset books i.e. the asset books are the records of all assets owned by the bank.

I asked him to explain to me in the context of a mortgage or other loan what the asset is. During this conversation I said to him: "I know the asset is not my house because according to the folio from the land registry office the property is 100% wholly and solely owned by me and is in my name and therefore it cannot be the asset".

I then commented, "The loan cannot be an asset because a loan is a big hole of nothingness and nothingness cannot be an asset, so can you please let me know what the asset is"?

I paused while I waited for his reply.

"..." He said nothing. He simply looked at me red faced and

'the asset is your signature'

appeared distinctly uncomfortable. Eventually he said: "That is the way it is and that is the way it has always been". Needless to say, that was not good enough for me. I was aware that just because that's the way it has always been done it does not mean that it is right.

Here is what I have discovered since; of course there is an asset and the asset is the 'borrowers' signature. Your signature was the instrument that was used to create security, money and contacts based on an understanding by the bank that in giving the signature the 'borrower' was giving his promise to give his life in service of the loan being agreed.

I soon realised that my signature had a power much greater than I had ever considered.

'signatures create money'

Why is my signature an asset?

Because your signature is a promise to pay; it is your promise to pay and along with everyone else's promise to pay that gives the banks the security they need to trade on the market and do all the buying and selling of the illusion that creates their perceived wealth. In effect the bank can go with all the signatures to the market place and say 'pardon me, but we have one million idiots (don't take that personally) who have made a commitment to go to work for the next forty years and give us a percentage of everything they earn, can we borrow money from you?'. Or furthermore, 'can we sell you their promise to pay; we will even act as the collection agent for you'. Their counterparts around the world say 'of course you can'. Your signature, (promise to pay), becomes the banks security to borrow from other banks and financial houses in the same way that your payslip acts as your security when you want to borrow for your house or car. Effectively, you are the payslip that the government or the bank needs to produce in order to show they have earning capacity. So your promise to pay is holding up the entire system worldwide. The banks simply exchange credit and create promises to pay deals, just like you did with your bank. In their credit trading moments no money is used or exists. They trade the idea of money, the perception of money but the money itself does not exist. A fantastic display of the power of a 'signature', the power of your signature, signatures create money!

So how did the bank bailout happen?

The bank bailout happened with the magic of the same perception and no actual money existed? Here is a quote from the answer of a parliamentary question by the Irish Minister for Finance, 'the capital (for the bailout) has been provided by the exchequer or the National Pension Fund (NPRF) by way of Promissory Notes...' (Parliamentary Questions 15/12/2011 ref: 40661/11) This answer tells us that no actual money was on the table in respect of the bank bailout... once again the system has played a game with the idea of money, the perception of money but that does not mean that actual money has been used. You are again lied to, mislead and misinformed.

Say more about 'signatures create money'?

Okay, let's take a step back for a moment. Remember if we all go into the bank for our money at the same time the bank will not have it to give to us. Now focus on what you think happens when you go in for your mortgage. You think the bank goes into its vault and takes out the €300,000.00 you are asking for and they lend it to you and you therefore owe the bank that money back plus interest, right? Wrong... that is not what happens. Remember the banks do not have the money to give to lend to everyone.

What does that mean?

It means what I said, when you go in for the loan the bank does not have the money to loan you.

So where does the money come from?

You create it, with your signature. Your signature is a promise to pay, so once you give the bank your promise to pay they create the credit according to the value of the agreed amount, in this case €300,000.00. That credit never existed before you walked into the bank but it does now because your signature created it. As you promised to pay the credit popped into existence.

Wow!, slow down... what does that mean?

It means that the bank knows you are going to head off and work for the next forty years to make money, once you have your money made each month you will kindly give it to them and hey presto! Money happens! They create money on a computer screen that is supported by your commitment to give them money in the future.

So I actually made money with my signature, I didn't borrow anything?
That is correct, now you are beginning to get it. You made the money, you did not borrow it. Take a moment to make sure you fully get what is happening here. You are learning that the banks have no money and never did. The money you believe you got to buy your house with was actually created by you.

So why do I owe the bank money if I created the money?
You don't owe them anything. How could you? As you just said yourself, you created the money.

So the government are aware of the business of how money works and the whole idea of creating money from nothing and making new money with promissory notes, is that correct?
Here is an article from the Independent Newspaper on February 9th 2012 entitled 'Promissory Note should be renegotiated, says Burton'...

> *"Minister for Social Protection Joan Burton said today that there is no reason why Ireland*

cannot get the terms of the repayment of a €31bn debt renegotiated.
Minister Burton was speaking at a gathering of Chartered Accountants in Dublin this afternoon.
The promissory note relates to funds that had to be injected into the former Anglo Irish Bank and Irish Nationwide.
Minister Burton said that it is up to the ECB to decide whether we can change the length of the repayment, to make it more affordable.
"We took out a €31bn promissory note, payable down in 10 years, now that's basically €3bn a year, which is the first call in terms of the resources of the State," "It's extremely onerous, it was probably a clever piece of financial engineering at the time, but there's no reason why it shouldn't be renegotiated, because it's essentially an I.O.U to ourselves - it's really an I-O-Me."

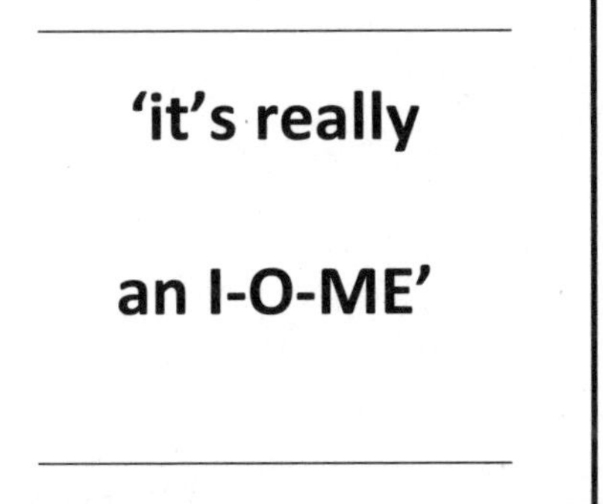

What does this tell you about what they know, what they do not know, what they understand and what they do not understand?

Let me clarify this, you are saying that I didn't borrow anything?
That is correct. You made the money, you did not borrow it.

Explain to me again why I owe the bank money if I created it?
You do not owe them anything.

Chapter 5

Full Disclosure

Did You Know

- Only 3% of all money is cash, the remaining 97% is fictional figures on a computer screen. The banks are broke and have nothing.

- Those responsible for governing the money game in Ireland are working for a European system whose priority is Europe, not Ireland. You are being traded and left with nothing so a few people at the top can own everything, including you.

- The only thing that makes the money game work is our participation. We can stop it, change it and create a new game that serves the people and not those who wish to perpetuate the cycle.

Will you explain how we can expose banks?

It begins with the promissory note which contains your signature. In depositing this note with the bank you loan them the value they put on the note. So let us say that you take out a mortgage for €300,000.00, with the promissory note being for the same amount. The bank then lodges it into their account and creates credit with it, with your signature having creating the money that has just been lodged. Although you think that you are borrowing money, the opposite is true, you are lending them the money that your signature has just created. In other words, the €300,000.00 did not exist before the promissory note was lodged, nor is credit transferred from their account to yours; rather it is new money that you created. This shows that money is created out of thin air and is dependent on our confidence to determine its worth. At this point the €300,000.00 will appear as digits on the computer screen. Congratulations, you have just created the mortgage that you have borrowed and will repay for the next three decades.

But I didn't give them money?

Are you sure? If I use a cheque to pay you one thousand euro for your car, did I give you money?

"Yes, I can deposit that cheque and the bank will honour it if there is money in your account to cover it. So within a few days the bank will transfer money to my account to the value of one thousand euro"

So when I gave you the cheque you believed you had money.
"Yes"
Consider the promissory note in the same way that you would a cheque. The promissory note is money, your money.

But you don't have the €300,000.00 in your account!
Wait a moment. Once I give the bank the promissory note it is deposited into the bank's account. This is one of the pieces of the puzzle that the bank does not inform you of. Once deposited, the promissory note becomes new money in their account. Because I deposited it with the bank I created the money to the value of the promissory note. In banking terms this means that my signature created the funds. So in reality I loaned the bank €300,000.00 and they repay me the €300,000.00. I own them nothing and they owe me nothing. Nothing was truly borrowed. We simply exchanged promissory notes and loans.

Can this be proven?
Just ask the bank to show you the bookkeeping entries for the transactions that occurred.

What will this show?
The bookkeeping entries will show that you created and loaned the bank the value of the promissory note.

What will the bank say?
They will tell you that the bank funded the loan, but the bookkeeping entries will prove that you funded the loan by creating new money with the deposit of your promissory note. Although the agreement you signed may suggest that the bank funded the loan, but the bookkeeping entries will show the opposite.

> **'Ask the bank to show you the bookkeeping entries'**

But what if they were dishonest in the entries?
The banks books will show what happened in terms of money coming in and going out. They will show that the bank loaned the borrower a bank liability which means that the bank owes the borrower money for the borrower's promissory note. Assuming that the bank lie about this, you will have to ask the right questions in order to uncover their true dealings i.e. money changing. Banks and bankers are money changers, nothing more.

I feel a bit confused, why do they open a liability book if I have given them money?

Try not to get confused by the trick of the game. Do you think that when you deposit money into the bank it is an asset for them?

"Yes, of course, it is in their bank, and it's their asset as long as they have it"

It is your money sitting in their account and therefore they owe it to you so it is a liability for the bank as much as it is an asset. Once you come looking for it they have to hand it over because it is your money. Remember that banking, like much of life is based on perception and not 'truth', like if you lodge €100 into your account it is logged as an asset; however, the bank creates a bank liability to the same value, which shows that they owe you the same amount. So, your lodgement causes an increase in the bank's asset and liability books to the same value. The bank's books must always balance so when something happens in one column something else must happen in the other column to balance it out. This is always the case... all you need now are the right questions to ask in order to understand the trickery that causes you to believe something is happening when it is not and that something completely different is taking place.

Explain what happens with the mortgage again slowly...

I sign a piece of paper that is a promissory note. That note is deposited into an account connected to the business of the transaction (that does not mean it is your account, only that it is deposited into an account where they drop all their deposits). Once deposited, the note creates new money to the value of the note; you know this new money to be credit! The bank in turn opens a liability book because they now owe you money to the value of the note; this bit you are not told and many in the bank have no idea why or how this happens or even the real meaning behind it. They simply do what they are told, they read from the script and they live from the assumption that it must be right because that is the way it has always been done...

> **'We simply exchanged promissory notes, we exchanged loans'**

Now the state of play is simple... you have funded the loan and they have repaid you what you have created. No true borrowing happened. You exchanged loans. You owe nothing and they owe nothing.

So I created the money and never borrowed anything at all? There is one thing that is bothering me, how come this has never been stopped or talked about?
Fear, conditioning, greed, fear, more fear, ignorance, arrogance, ego, fear, more fear, more fear, more ignorance, more fear. We have created a world where the abnormal has become the norm. The world we live

says it is ok and normal to get drunk to the point of falling over and when talking about it people actually say 'it was a great night'. The world we live in says it is ok that a church can be responsible for the rape of thousands of young children and continue in business without being run down, run out and run over. The world we live in says it is ok to medicate people for mental illnesses that the medical world knows don't exist; we diagnose people with mental illness that don't even have medical definitions. The world we live in can allow the American and British defence forces occupy someone else's land, kill their people, rape their women, steal their natural resources and do so backed up only by a bunch of lies and made-up stories about weapons of mass destruction that never existed and after the world finds out they were lying we sit back as they continue to murder, rape and steal from these countries and we do nothing.

These things happen because we are ignorant as to who we are, what life is really all about and what our true nature really is. These things happen because we choose not to have powerful, honest and open conversations. These things happen because we choose not to challenge and change our belief systems.

But the banks will insist that you owe the money?

Of course they will, but read the agreement and see what it says and then measure it alongside the finance standards, codes of practice and regulation criteria. You will see that they are only tricksters. That being said it seems their hiding places may not be so safe anymore.

How can I get an experience of what you are saying?
That is a very exciting question for you to ask because there is a difference between understanding something and experiencing it. As soon as you begin to ask powerful questions the bank will realise that you are no longer afraid and they will become afraid of you, at which point, they will know that the game of smoke and mirrors is up. Just think of the magician Darren Brown, who as a master of illusion shows that amazing things can appear to happen when all that is really happening is trickery of the most basic kind. It just looks impressive but only because you know so little about how it is done. Once you know the trick and you catch the deception as it happens the magic is gone and the illusion is bust.

So what can I ask them that will get a response in my favour?
Try the following few questions for a start, have fun with it. It is better to ask these face to face because then you can see the reaction and experience the flow of life rise up in you as the banker fumbles in a state of no grace.

1. What is the asset that you lodged?
2. Did you open a liability book in relation to the asset?
3. What is the legal and lawful definition of the term 'money' in relation to our agreement?
4. Did the bank use the promissory note as money or the equivalent to fund the loan?

5. What are the financial standards and regulations that you are required to follow by law in relation to lending?
6. What do those standards say in relation to depositing assets and opening an asset and liability book in relation to the same?
7. Who or what is the bank?
8. Who is the person legally responsible for and legally representing the bank in relation to these matters?
9. What was the true intention behind the agreement from the banks perspective and in relation to the bank's true nature of business?
10. Do the bank's articles and memorandums of association allow for it to do business in the way it is doing it?
11. Did the borrower provide the funding capital for the loan to the same borrower?
12. Is it true that the bank creates money when they lend money?
13. Considering that the bank has hidden the loan that was made to the bank when the promissory note was lodged, is this not stealing, fraud and misrepresentation?
14. Are all of the people who were involved in my original 'loan' agreements with the bank fully compliant with the financial regulator's demands for them to be trained and qualified to the appropriate standards, and are they in receipt of the proper certificates that prove they have passed the exams that allow them to 'sell' money?

15. What are the terms and conditions of the banks licence in relation to the process of lending and using promissory notes to fund lending?

Once the banks have answered these questions, which they will not, ask them to sign an affidavit swearing to the answers; which they will also refuse to do, but watch what happens when you push for a signed statement standing by the same. And watch what happens when you arm yourself with these questions and many more and you let the bank know you will take this process into court and publically seek the answers with the courts order.

Surely there is someone in the banks that would be happy to tell the truth of what is going on?

There are a number of levels within the bank and when you understand these levels you will understand why nobody is talking. The first level is comprised of those who know exactly what is going on, how it is happening and what the logic behind it is. These people are not talking because they are protecting the life they have created for themselves. They are stuck in the belief that they are right and what they do is in accordance with the natural order of things. They also live in a world where their ego is significant and their narcissistic view of themselves is such that they have lost sight of anything that is real, grounded and value based. The next level is that of their minions who aspire to be like those they work for. They live from a sense of insecurity so thick and solid that all they see is the potential glory of pleasing those they believe hold a god-like position. They are drunk on the validation they get and are so desperate for more that they are willing to sell their souls to get it. Many are aware of what is going on but the fear of not being 'somebody' is far greater than the risk of exposing the truth and losing the dream of having the power that their life has taught them is so important to have. Remember, many of these people were raised to believe that power equals success, success equals happiness and happiness equals having 'made it'.

The third level includes the people who have found themselves in a job that provides security and a steady income; we could call them the front of house staff. These people dream of having a nice pension and a happy retirement and they have convinced themselves that they are helping people in providing them with funds to buy all the things in the world that make us happy. Of course, they rarely if ever stop long enough to ask and answer the most important questions in life as they know deep down that if they do a lot of change will follow, this change will bring uncertainly and in uncertainly there is a risk of being vulnerable and vulnerability is not something many people know how to do well.

The people at the top of the ladder have salaries, benefits and bonuses that they cannot imagine living without. They are stuck in the fear of not having enough and feel they need to increase their bank accounts in order to believe they are somebody important. It is not unusual for a top banking official to earn in a single month what the average person earns in an entire year. On top of this, they have annual bonuses to protect, lifestyles to maintain and people to impress. Many of them also benefit from 'behind closed doors' benefits and secret remuneration packages. They get to connect with the high positioned people of society and experience the things of fantasy that most people do not even know exists.

For some of these people there is no limit to what they will do to protect their world and they are willing to throw you, your children and your life dreams to the wolves. Their ego state is responsible for finding new ways of manipulating the world in order to become even wealthier, and even when they get there, it is never enough. It is this mentality that is responsible for creating industries and wars that tear our world apart, cut down our planets plant life and drive the indigenous people from their homes. It is a potentially depressing truth but some of these people are a chip off the block of all that is bad and wrong with the world.

Who is governing them?

Nobody. All the right organisations are in place with a list of policies and procedures but they are all dominated by cronies from the industry. They are all fed by the same hand and none are willing to cut off their food supply.

Here is an excerpt from an answer to a parliamentary question that addresses this issue. Irish Parliamentary Question ref: 40661/11, responded to by The Minister for Finance December 2011.

"A number of bodies including the Department of Finance, the Central Bank and the Financial Regulator and the EU Commission are directly involved in monitoring the performance and compliance of various institutions on an on-going basis"

This tells us that nobody is governing the banks from the perspective of protecting, supporting and helping the Irish people. The Department of Finance is on the side of Europe and is controlled by the Troika. The Financial Regulator is essentially the Central Bank of Ireland which has the Minister for Finance as its only shareholder and is a part 'owner' of the European Central Bank which has no concern for Ireland as a sovereign nation. Furthermore, the EU Commission is the executive body of the European Union and its job is to uphold the treaties of the European Union. In fact, when making decisions under the umbrella of the EU Commission, Irish politicians must decide for the good of the union and not allow Ireland to be prioritised.

But is there no one to highlight that the agreements these people are selling are unfair and downright fraud?

They write the agreements and sanction the contents along with the governing bodies that are in the game with them. It only appears that they are separate but they are all one and the same. Every branch of the tree is entangled with every other branch and everyone is afraid to stand up because they know that they can be held

responsible for what is happening. Governments, Banks, Religious Establishments, Health Systems, the Medical Industry, Systems of Education and the Legal Profession are all run at the highest level by people who are disconnected from any true meaning, all other people else in the system are simply the foot soldiers that carry out the orders and ensuring not to question anything for fear of losing their job. Those at the higher levels are like vampires who feed off the life blood, energy and good will of a population who dream of community and peace.
There is no transparency or honesty in the banking system nor is there a desire to set people free. It is merely an illusion that is powered by fear, greed, ignorance, bullying, duality, control, poverty consciousness, lies, deceit and misrepresentation. The truth needs to be exposed so we can change our beliefs, create a better experience of life for all (even the bankers), learn the true nature of life, experience oneness, recognise our potential, realise that we are the creating force of life and live in and from love.

What if they say that I owe them the money?
Tell them that you now know that it was you who funded the capital for the loan when your promissory note was monetised and deposited in the bank. Use the bookkeeping records to prove your case. They will show that you lodged with the bank note that was monetised to the value of the figure on the note. The liability book also shows that the bank was clear in its understanding that they owed you the value of the transaction and the

handing over of the check was the settling of the debt to you.

I don't fully understand what you mean by 'asset' and liability. Can you explain it further?

Let us look at a section of an affidavit of WALKER F. TODD, expert witness for defendants in the case of A BANK v HARSHAVARDHAN DAVE and PRATIMA DAVE (Defendants), State of Michigan.

David H. Friedman, MONEY AND BANKING (4th ed. 1984)

> *""the commercial bank lending process is similar to that of a thrift in that the receipt of cash from depositors increases both its assets and its deposit liabilities, which enables it to make additional loans and investments... when a commercial bank makes a business loan, it accepts as an asset the borrower's debt obligation (the promise to repay) and creates a liability on its books in the form of a demand deposit in the amount of the loan" Customer loans are funded similarly). Therefore, the bank's original bookkeeping entry should show an increase in the amount of asset credited on the asset side of its books and a corresponding increase equal to the value of the asset on the liability side of its books. This would show that the bank received the customer's signed promise to repay as an asset, thus monetizing the customer's signature and creating on its books a liability in the form of a demand or other demand liability of the bank. The bank then usually would*

hold this demand deposit in a transaction account on behalf of the customer. Instead of the bank lending its money or other assets to the customer, as the customer reasonably might believe from the face of the Note, the bank created funds to the customer's transaction account without the customer's permission, authorization, or knowledge and delivered the credit on its own books representing those funds to the customer, meanwhile alleging that the bank lent the customer money. If the Plaintiff's response to this line of argument is to the effect that it acknowledges that it lent credit or issued credit instead of money, one might refer to Thomas P. Fitch, BARRON'S BUSINESS GUIDE DICTIONARY OF BANKING TERMS, "Credit banking," 3. "Bookkeeping entry representing a deposit of funds into an account". But Plaintiff's loan agreement apparently avoids claiming that the bank actually lent the Defendants money. They apparently state in the agreement that the defendants are obligated to repay Plaintiff principal and interest for the "Valuable consideration (money) the bank gave the customer (borrower)". The loan agreement and Note apparently still delete any reference to the bank's receipt of actual cash value from the Defendants and exchange of that receipt for actual cash value that the Plaintiff banker returned."

So, I am an asset not a liability, is that right?

Correct, how could you be anything else? The true nature of your entire existence is that of 'creator'. You create your income, children, relationships, and your fitness level. You create the plans for your home and the opportunity that allows you to build it. You create the changes in your life and the experience of connection to whatever God you believe in. You create your understanding of life's challenges and the way through your own personal struggles. You create your mind set, focus, luck and all that is needed to tap into your potential, as well as the resistance that prevents you from realising your dreams. You create the fear that gets you stuck in life and the discomfort that makes you anxious and stressed. If you are not the one in charge of your life who is? Of course, you are an asset to the bank, without you they do not exist.

What if all this information collapses the system and we end up with nothing?

But you have nothing now. This is one of the most important things you must realise in order to get past step one in this process of re-educating yourself. All you have now is the illusion that with hard work, great effort and some luck at the far end of a heart attack or a brush with cancer you will end up with something. But the truth is that you will end up with nothing as long as you continue to play the game that the illusion is built upon. What you need to do is to allow the illusion to fade away so that you are left with nothing but the truth of who you are. From here you can build a life that brings you what matters most; Peace. After all why are so many people getting into 'debt'... because they hope that at some stage they will be able to feel peace.

Surely the banks didn't lie to me, did they?

Before I answer that question let me ask you a question: who is the bank? Have you noticed how 'The Bank' threatens you in all the letters that you receive. They threaten to take you to court, repossess your home, lift your overdraft and stop your credit facilities if you do not do what they say? But who is this bank that is behaving like this? It is an entity that does not breathe, walk, talk, earn, make telephone calls or write letters. The banking 'reality' (pardon the use of the word 'reality' in this context) is built within a system that is comprised of beliefs, rules, regulations, processes, procedures, internal (more) systems, structures, strategies and traditional understandings that have been handed down through the generations. It is not there to help you, nor does it exist to make life easier. Its function is not to support you, show understanding or compassion. The beliefs, processes, systems and strategies of the bank all support one outcome which is to make money by taking

> **'What you really need now is to become disillusioned'**

from you what you have. Do not be fooled into thinking that they care because they gave you a loan or helped you buy a new car. They only gave you what they did so that they could take it off you and on top of that add a charge. They give you money (the illusion of money) in order to take it back, plus interest.

So the system is simply doing what the system does in order to achieve what it was designed to do. They claim they are not lying to you and that they are there to help but the experience says different. So, is the bank lying to you? YES, because it is not being honest but from its perspective NO because it believes its own rubbish. It has bought into and learned to believe its own publicity.

Recently I had a meeting with a young woman called Michelle in one of the main banks in Ireland. I was there with Paul, who was trying to find a way out of his current difficulties with his home mortgage. Remember the bank cannot talk, so Michelle is the bank when she speaks on behalf of the bank's concerns or interest in the matter.

Paul asked for a write-down on a certain percentage of the mortgage in order to find a way forward. Without thinking, she responded 'we don't do write-downs on residential, only commercial'. Paul then enquired about his options. Michelle (with a straight, emotionless and cold expression) responded 'we will request that you sell the house, we will take the proceeds and the balance of the loan that remains you will be responsible for'.

As you can imagine Paul was not happy with this response and stated that he would not be selling the house as it was his family home. Michelle further explained that they would bring it through the court system and from there it would be sold, the proceeds would pay off a certain amount of the loan and the balance would still be owed by Paul. I then asked the question 'where is Paul and his family supposed to live and how are they supposed to manage in life if their house is gone, they have a big balance to pay off and there is no income.' Michelle's response was... wait for it! "Well, at that stage I am sure Paul and his family will qualify for social housing"

You wonder if the banks care about you. The banks do not care. They are in the business of making money and they will do so even if it means that you lose everything. If a person in the bank begins to explore a more humanistic approach to what they do, they are

---

'the system that controls them has no compassion, no understanding and no desire to become compassionate or to understand'

---

either moved to a non client facing position or they lose their job. That is the nature of the system, and unfortunately many people within the system become consumed with fear and in order to protect their job, income and home they are content to work in denial of what they are doing.

Then there is Ita, the 82 year old woman who was given a mortgage at 76 years of age to help her son, and is now under threat from the banks because she cannot repay it, so much so that it looks like she may lose her home, or Teresa, who was given €13,000,000.00 in mortgages in the last ten years and at 76 years old risks losing everything, including her health because she is suffering from depression. There is also Mark, who has lost his job, his home and his relationship. His wife and children are living with her parents and he has developed a drink problem, and I have not even mentioned the people who have hanged themselves, or the men who have used a gun to shoot a hole in their body in the hope of escaping their fear of the bank. Why not answer your own question 'do the banks care about you'?

The question I have for you is a simple one.
Do you care about you?

Chapter 6

Awake From Your Slumber

Did You Know

- Banks get away with what they do by keeping you living in fear of them. The truth is they have no power over you, unless you allow it.
- Ignorance is your greatest weakness and educating yourself is your greatest strength.
- If you remain asleep, silent and fearful, your future will be one of pain and suffering. It is time to waken up.

How are the banks getting away with this?

How many times have you heard people talk about the level of disbelief they are living with in relation to what is happening and how it can be allowed to continue? The stories in circulation are overwhelming. There are many reasons why it is happening but the most powerful resource that the banks have can be summed up in three words: ignorance, fear and disempowerment.

By 'ignorance' do you mean that we are stupid?
No, I mean that we are living under a set of beliefs that keep us blind. We have been badly informed and are living without being conscious of what 'living' means. There is much more to life than getting up in the morning, going to work, paying the bills and going to bed in order to get up and do it all over again. Life is an incredibly complex experience and it involves our physical, intellectual, spiritual and emotional input. To claim that you are alive and fully engaging in life there needs to be an embrace of all aspects of the self and all the experiences that life has to offer.

Is it really important to know ourselves when dealing with the banks?
Yes, it is. I listen to people every day explain what is going on in their lives in relation to their difficulties with the bank. The words, statements and questions that arise most often in these conversations include: I'm afraid, angry and scared. I don't know what to do. I can't

believe I am in this situation. How did this happen? What is all this about? Is there a way out of this? What is going to happen next? Can it get any worse? I don't want to live anymore. I feel so stupid. I am such an idiot. Is there anything good that can come from this? What is the purpose in life? I just want to make all this go away. What will happen if I end up in court? What did I do to deserve this? Surly there is more to life than this? I have never been so close to losing everything before? What have I been working for? How am I supposed to feed my children and pay the bills? I just don't see a way forward. I'm so depressed. My husband is not himself anymore. My children are picking up on all the tension. Please help me to understand what I am to do now.

'banks at the moment are behaving in a way that is making a lot of people feel very unsafe, vulnerable and worthless'

Look closer at these questions and statements. See how they are not just concerned with the banking issue, but with the bigger picture of life. It seems that people are looking for something to make them feel safe, rather than threatened and exposed. Threatened, because the banks have the power to take everything people have worked for, and exposed because we realise that we have nothing outside the bank's reach. Furthermore, the government, revenue system and legal system regularly punish those who stand before a judge when all they are looking for is support and help.

So because we live with this ignorance, we do not have the resources or knowledge to do anything about it, correct?

Yes, because so many people live in ignorance, no one can figure out what to do next. After all, the power of ignorance comes from the fact that you do not know what you do not know. How can you find a way forward if you don't know what you need to know to move forward? It is this ignorance then drives people to look to someone else who they believe has the power to do what they cannot do. So they end up knocking on the door of a solicitor or barrister, and once the door is opened the person lets go of any chance they had of getting what they need. Initially, we gave our power to the banks, and now we are transferring it to the legal profession. At this stage, the solicitor tells us what they can and cannot do and why that is so, which means that the solicitor now becomes the one who creates your future whilst taking from you the few euro you have left.

Maybe the solicitor is their only hope; after all they are afraid of losing their business, their savings and their home?

As I mentioned earlier 'fear' is one of the most powerful things that a bank has working in their favour and they use it to make sure that you do not get too confident.

What are people so afraid of?

We are afraid of getting it wrong, of screwing up and being judged. We are afraid of the 'authority' figures, of what we think they know and of disappointing our families. We are afraid of having nothing, of not knowing what to say, when to say it and who to say it to. We are afraid of being laughed at or seen as having failed. Fear is one of the most powerful experiences a person can have. It will drive them to drink or drugs, to run away or to breakdown, to lose their mind, to lie, to cheat, to murder and to suicide. Fear, if it is allowed will consume a person's life and can eventually bring that person to a place of total reliance upon external factors that will compel them to live out someone else's belief system.

Try to remember a time in your life when you felt fear and you will begin to understand what many people are experiencing on a daily bases. Can you feel how it permeates every aspect of your life, your physical and mental health, your relationships your rest time, your vision for the future and your desire to believe that there is hope and your energy levels? Can you understand how fear is undermining our trust in people and driving us into a state of paralysis where we find ourselves unable to move in any direction? Now can you see how fear is the most powerful tool that the banks have against you? Do they not tell you that if you do not do what they what and when they want that they will take you to court and the legal system will commit you to a life of repayments, even if you cannot afford them and from this to jail if you do not pay? Fear is a child of ignorance and as long as you are living without the knowledge of who you are you will live in fear of what is going to happen to you. Is this what you dreamed of as a child and a young adult, a life of fear?

Where does the fear come from?

It is essentially programmed into you as a child. You were shouted at when you did something 'wrong' or said something 'inappropriate'. You were told how to behave by the policeman and reprimanded by the teacher. You felt humiliated when someone hit you and you were shamed when someone abused you. You are laughed at when you are not cool enough and felt deeply saddened when your parents did not connect with you, encourage or support you. You may even have been horrified by thoughts of God abandoning you to the devil if you committed sin. The fear we meet in our lives comes from particular moments in our development many of which are so powerful that they hard wire us to a life of avoidance where we live in dread of experiencing the circumstances that MAY cause us to revisit these feelings of hurt, shame, humiliation or fear. That is why fear is so powerful.

So if I live in ignorance, which is a state of 'not knowing who I truly am', will I live in fear?

Yes. Fear will cause you to experience a life of disempowerment to such an extent that you will feel unable to change the things that are not working, effect what is holding you back or let go of all that is choking you. You will know you are in a disempowered state when you fear the banks, another person's opinion of you or when you believe that someone else has something that you do not have and without it you cannot be happy nor can you be at peace.

Being disempowered is like being anesthetised, where you are numbed from enjoying the freedom, energy or mindfulness to live life according to what you want for yourself. Instead of which, you will live the life that the world dictates even though you know it is not what you want.

So what can I do?

Disempowerment is fuelled by the fear borne out of ignorance, so in order to be free you need to know who you truly are, what is your life's purpose and from there create a new set of values which begins with the commitment to change your beliefs which in turn, changes your behaviour. There is little point in changing your behaviour first because there will develop an internal conflict that will cause you to default back to your original state.

So, in relation to the banks, you will awaken to your true self by realising that money is an illusion, the banking world is a game, and 'debt' does not exist. As you begin to consider this and hear these ideas become aware of the resistance you feel and the internal voices that will challenge you to remain stuck in the fear.

Are you saying that I am asleep?

Are you afraid? Do you live in a world where you need to defend yourself all the time? Is your life one of peace or chaos? Do you spend your time trying to please other people? Are you spending your life working in a job that you hate? Do you wake up most mornings filled with excitement, or dread? Do you live according to the labels the world puts on you?

Where is all this going?

If you refuse to look beyond what the 'authority' figures of the world tell you is reality, then you will be led deeper into the place you find yourself in now and feel more entrenched in the mindset that you are powerless to do anything and that you will eventually end up with nothing. Can you see the irony? You are afraid of the system, to stand up to it and admit that it does not care about you, because you fear that you will end up with nothing when in fact you have nothing now (the system has it all), and even if you do find a 'way forward' with the bank, the system will eventually take everything anyway.

Let me explain why. For the bank, a way forward is a payment plan that allows you to pay them what they need for as many years as it is going to take to repay all that you own; the arrears you are currently in, the interest on the arrears, the interest that has yet to be added onto your outstanding balance plus all the charges that will be incurred. While doing this you are also expected to feed and clothe yourself, heat your home, provide for your children, pay medical bills and organise a holiday every so often. You have to provide for birthdays, Christmases, and other special occasions. Eventually you will be left only with debt and a life with no time, money, energy or freedom.

Did we not create all this by taking too much and being greedy?

There is no doubt that greed played a part in what happened to the economy in Ireland and all the other countries around the world. However, it is unfair to say that everyone was greedy and this created the whole mess. It is more accurate to say that all some people did was to dream of rising above their sense of struggle. For most of the population the 'new found wealth' was the chance to buy a home or to extend the home they already had. For others, it was an opportunity to invest in a holiday home or realise the dream of owning their own business. What is wrong with that? Doubtless, in some cases it did get out of hand, but before we knew it the entire country was so far into the game that there was no chance of getting out. Then the bubble burst and here we are now. Let us look at a few other reasons how we ended up in the current position:

Lifting limits on lending

The people who decide what is fair and balanced in terms of lending money lifted their limits and this allowed a significant amount of lending to happening way above what was manageable. They knew where it would lead but most of the population trusted that those in the 'know' were managing everything and making sure things stayed safe, most believed that things would be fine, why wouldn't they?

Dishonesty

The banks and financial institutions were not honest with their customers. They did not tell the truth in terms of the nature of their business, where the money was coming from, what the consequences were if things continued, nor were they honest in disclosing what people were legally and lawfully entering into as they allegedly borrowed vast amounts of money.

Hidden Agendas

Governments used the illusion of wealth to buy voter confidence for the purpose of staying in office where they continued playing their games at a much higher level with more significant sums of the illusionary money.

Personal Gain

Senior and middle management in the banks were making vast sums of money in sales commission and it suited them to continue selling money in the form of loans, credit cards, car finance packages, overdrafts and other financial investment opportunities, all of which supported their lavish lifestyles. They didn't care about the outcomes, if they did we would not be in the position we are in now.

International Approval

In order to gain approval from the 'European Powers' i.e. decision makers, European countries had to look economically strong. Once a high credit rating was achieved, they were considered well positioned for financial investment from supporting funds, commercial investment and tourism incentives etc. As a result, countries like Ireland borrowed enormous amount of money and in doing so took their eye off the ball in terms of what mattered most, the people. Enough was never enough, and all the time our plans to create a great country based on financial wealth were planting the seeds of our own destruction.

Blind Puppets

Ireland tried to play a game that was not ours to play and the government at the time were too ignorant, arrogant and stupid to see that they were being played for the benefit of the world's corporate giants. They were too full of their own importance to realise that their eventual going bust would be insignificant to the big game players.

The Bigger Picture

The global wealth that was being created was used to fund the wars that are required to allow the superpower(s) to eliminate the nations that were in disagreement with their arrogance and god complex. As we were all distracted with our new lives, hundreds of thousands of people were being 'put in their place' by being forced to enter the ultimate game of life.

I have never given much consideration to some of the things you are talking about here!

Many people go through life without asking the most important questions. They enjoy life's pleasures and bare life's pain without much reflection on what it all means. So for these people, the exposure of the great banking con game will fall on deaf ears, most likely filtered through old beliefs that will cause them to respond 'that's terrible', but nothing more. The possibility of entertaining new information is so challenging that we often chose not to take it on board. Our fear of discovering that we have been living in a world that operates differently to the one we have been led to believe is 'right' is nothing less than frightening for many who feel under resourced to cope with this paradigm shift.

Imagine that the fundamental beliefs you hold in life are like legs on a chair and such is your dependence on the chair that without it you would collapse. Imagine someone comes along with a saw and threatens to cut one of the legs. Will you allow them to remove one of the few fundamental elements of your reality? Of course not, in fact, you will defend the chair because without that leg you will no longer feel supported and the chair might collapse.

Out of the fear that our life (chair) will become unstable we defend the banking system. We blame the government, greed and the bankers, but we do not consider that the belief itself might be wrong. We then start looking for a way out, but the way out we are looking for is not really a way out only a new way back in again. So, imagine that someone is in debt to the sum of one million euro and they cannot repay it. They begin to realise that something is wrong and that the future is not looking like the dream they once had. They stand up and say "I want out of this mess". The bank agrees to reduce their debt to four hundred thousand euro and the person accepts the offer. Although it will be difficult to repay, it is considerable less than the original amount. They then re-enter life believing they have escaped from the monster and tell people how lucky they are having come so close to having nothing and celebrating the fact that they can now get back to normal.

Watch the trick of the game...

Give a man two options; one that is impossible to achieve and the other that is possible. Obviously the man will choose the latter. As he gets excited about the possibility of breaking out of the prison of that which is unachievable and musters up the energy to grab the easier option he does not realise that there exists a third option. In fact, life says that there are many more options than just one and two but he is so distracted by that to which his attention has been brought that he fails to see anything else. So he focuses on the success of the less damaging option and all the time misses the other options that could resolve his problem permanently.

What's option three?
Pay only what you have to, not what the bank say you must pay or pay nothing because you own nothing.

So I let them cut the leg of my chair?
Yes.

And then what, I can't sit on the chair anymore?
Yes, but would you want to continue sitting in a life that is managed by a set of rules designed to keep you ignorant, fearful and disempowered?

But just because one leg is bad it does not mean the other legs are bad, does it? So if the legs of the chair represent the fundamental pillars of life and one leg represents the finance world and the banking reality, what do the other legs of your chair (life) represent?
Church/Religion, the Law/Legal System, Health Service & Education system. So let me ask you a few questions. The fundamental belief that your religion is the one true way to God and that the priest holds that special position of truth, knowledge and goodness and through him you are connected to God... how does that stack up when you consider the amount of priests who have abused children. It doesn't stack up very well, does it? What about your belief that the legal system exists to protect you and to make sure that no one takes from you what is

yours? How does that stack up, considering you recently lost your business to the banks and in the near future there is a good chance you will lose your home? It doesn't stack up very well, does it?

Then there is the health service. Do you believe that the world of doctors, medicine and pharmaceuticals is saving lives and helping people to be better, happier, and healthier? There are many powerful schools of thoughts that suggest that the health service kills people, makes others dependent on drugs and treats the illness without addressing the reasons behind it. That doesn't stack up either does it?

Do not forget the education system which has to be held accountable considering the number of 'teachers' who have held government office in the past. Coupled with the fact that the current head of government, continues to dig Ireland into a big hole, was also a teacher in his previous incarnation. And we haven't even begun to talk about the lack of life skills taught in schools in this country. It is all about high grades, getting big jobs and becoming a part of the machine that is mostly suffocating and killing a true and real quality of life. It looks like you might be better off sitting on the floor.

If this is the case, what do you trust or believe in?

Yourself and your limitless potential! You believe in your community and in the power of the collective to create a better future. You believe in the truth that you can dream a future and a new experience of life and you can then do what is needed to ensure that it comes about as your living experience.

But I am starting to think that I have no idea who I am?

Without knowing who you are, or at least starting to ask the right questions you have no chance of understanding the true nature of the illusion of the banks and the monetary system. I could go through all that I have learned with you, but it needs to be understood in the context of the bigger picture.

But I feel lost now!

That is only because the information is new, and you are learning that your life is something other than what you thought it was. Quite soon you will know exactly what you need to know in order change the experience of life from what it is to what you need it to be.

Are there practical things that I can do to deal with the banking stuff?

I will take you through that later but first of all I will tell you more about the banks themselves, the legal system, how this game came about, how it is played and where you can find the way out once and for all.

Chapter 7

Who Is 'The Bank'

Did You Know

- The bank needs you to be in debt to succeed.
- The banks are running the government and the government lives in fear of their power.
- The bank does not care if you live or die.

Is it possible to expose the bank's criminal activity?
Yes. However, it will take a nation of people standing together to ensure that the banks and the government who are covering for them are held responsible to the point of creating change. Once we come together we will have our power back.

Can I ask you what might seem like a stupid question?
Of course you can but remember there are no stupid questions. However, you demonstrate a good example of why the system is winning. People are afraid to ask questions because society has taught them that not knowing answers mean they are stupid.

What is a bank?
A bank is a business that has been carefully crafted and powerfully resourced in order to ensure that its outcomes are achieved. A bank is also an institution that is built upon layers of policies, procedures and structures that are virtually impossible to penetrate if you are one of the sheeple. The true purpose of a bank is to make money by buying and selling money or what we now know is the illusion of money.

What is a sheeple?
The people who act like sheep and follow instructions from those they choose to believe know more than they do. The sheeple are the people who go through life asleep but thinking they are awake, they don't think for

themselves, they defend the very system that is keeping them numb and they dismiss anyone that tries to tell them things can be different.

So, where do the banks get all the money from to buy and sell?

Banks create money in different ways. Remember that money does not equal cash. Albeit that money is cash, it is much more than that. Some of the terms used to describe what money is include:

Legal Tender
Cash
Promissory Notes
Lawful Money
Cheques
Credit
I.O.U's
Currency
Bank Money

In short, anything can be used as money once all the people involved in the transaction accept the given 'thing' in exchange for the goods or services. However, the general public more often than not do not look beyond the idea of cash as being money. Banks trade money in many different forms. They make money on charges to your account for administration and associated costs in keeping your account up to date. They also make money buying and selling bonds, investments, insurance policies, saving schemes, current accounts, deposits of cash, promissory notes, buying and selling precious metals, investing in other companies and organisations. The list goes on. The bankers are masters of the money game and they know how to make as much as possible from any given reality that is laid before them. They also make money from selling your loans and turning them into stock for the market to trade with and they rap all this up in the wonderful world of fractional reserve banking, which is the greatest illusion of all.

Who are the people behind the banks?

All you will find behind the banks are other banks and organisations. The amount of forensic work that would have to be done to answer that question is so enormous that it would take more money, people power, legal pull, government intervention and time than we could comprehend. This is how the banks can do what they do and get away with it. Take an example of a customer having a problem with their account. Let us assume that one hundred euro has gone missing from his account. He will have to call the bank many times before he will find someone who can rectify the problem. He will also have to send letters, copies of statements and explanations of what he believes has gone wrong. He will most likely have to fill in a number of standard internal process documents to get action to be taken in order for the problem to be addressed including; complaint forms, request for refund forms, signed agreements and disclaimer forms. After all this he may or may not get a satisfactory conclusion and if he does not he will be forced to go to a regulatory body or an ombudsman in order to have the matter examined. If the numbers involved in the problem are small enough the customer may get so swamped in the procedures that he eventually lets it go with a whimper of how unforgiving, cold and mean hearted the banking system is. He then continues on with his life not knowing who was responsible, how the problem occurred in the first place nor with an understanding of how it should have been dealt with.

It appears that the greater the problem, the thicker the layers of administration that exist, and the more complex the procedures are to find the cause. Meanwhile the customer is spending time, energy, personal resources and even money (if legal people are involved) in order to fix a problem that hides within a system that was designed to hide things and achieve the only goal it was meant to achieve; to increase its profit margins.

But that does not tell me who the banks are?

Of course not. We know who the bank manager is and who works at the front desk. We are familiar with the CEO and the names of all those on the board but the bank itself is an enigma. The bank is simply a company that is registered in a country (or not) that follows policies and procedures in order to do what it was designed to do. Everything else is a part of the game it plays to keep the truth from people.

What truth?

That the banks are in business to create and sell money and your involvement is to help them make more money. What the bank is not is an organisation that is concerned with your future. They are only there to 'lend' you money by convincing you that money is actually real and necessary, so that you can pay it back, plus interest and charges as well as the penalties and at the end, and if you ever get to the end they will 'lend' you more because they know you are good for another few years.

You want to buy a house valued at €300,000.00 and the bank 'lend' you the money. Over the next 30 years you pay off the loan at the principal rate plus interest and the charges that they dictate, and at the end of that period you have paid over €600,000.00. In order for you to pay off that alleged loan you will need to earn in excess of €1,000,000.00. How is that fair? Does that sound like you are being helped? Of course everyone wants to know 'what choice have I got?' Well there are options available but the general public are not educated in such matters.

For you to be able to service the mortgage you will need to invest somewhere in the region of €33,000.00 (gross) per year, and all that before you eat, pay for your car, clothe yourself, have a holiday, enjoy a hobby, pay your bills, tax, insure and fuel your car, insure, furnish and maintain your home, take up a course of study, pay your medical insurance and bills, have a meal out, cover the cost of special 'occasions', buy coal for the fire and cover unexpected expenses. This excludes the cost of having children; clothes, food, toys, games, days out, hospitals and doctors, day care, school, college, Christmas, birthdays, and those special days in the children's life that often have a high price attached to them.

The bank likes you to feel that they, through their loan facilities are the source of the funds that you need in order to make this unending experience of spending possible. The truth is that the borrowing of money that is attached to an interest rate is the reason that these things are almost impossible to manage. Imagine what it would be like to pay your mortgage if there was no interest on the payments?

> **'the current regime that Ireland is experiencing is closer to an unhealthy communist or fascist regime'**

Is there no governing body to stop the banks doing what they do and to make sure that what they do is fair and right?

The first thing is that fair and right are not words that describe anything the banks are involved in otherwise the economy would not be in the shape it is in. That being said, look at how the system is built. In Ireland the main commercial banks are mostly government owned, or are claimed to be owned by the people. However, if we were truly their owners, everything would change, but it is the government that runs things, and it is merely a puppet of the European and world systems. Although we pepper our language with terms like "democracy" and "republic" when discussing our nation, their reiteration does mirror the fact that our government and how it does business more resembles a communist or fascist regime.

The reality of the situation is that the banks are under the guidance of the Central Bank of Ireland and are privately owned and run in accordance with the desires of their senior directors, all of whom are in the business of making money for their shareholders. In a recent conversation with a member of staff in the Central Bank who is employed to answer the questions that people like me and you might put forward this is what I was told:

Question: Is the Central Bank publicly owned?

Answer: No

Question: Is the Central Bank privately owned?

Answer: No

Question: If it is not publicly owned or privately owned who owns it?

Answer: There is no definitive answer to that.

Question: Are you telling me that your answer to the question who owns the central bank of Ireland is 'there is no definitive answer?

Answer: Yes

Question: So are the employees of the Central Bank Civil Servants?

Answer: No

Question: Are they public servants?

Answer: No

Question: Are they employed the same as someone in a private organisation.

Answer: It's hard to say, I guess so but not exactly

Question: How do I get a definitive answer to these questions?

Answer: There is none really but I would suggest you check out our website.

Question: Who are the shareholders of the Central Bank?

Answer: The bank has only one shareholder

Question: Who is that?

Answer: The current Minister for Finance

Question: Are you saying that the Minster for Finance is the sole shareholder of an organisation that is not a public company?

Answer: He is the only shareholder

Question: Is there a board of directors in the Central Bank

Answer: No, there is a commission

Question: Are they elected by the government or voted into place?

Answer: They are positioned by the government

Question: Are any of them now or have any of them been at one point people of significant position in government appointed jobs and positions of 'national interest'

Answer: Yes.. I will call out their names and positions for you.

A number of days later I received an email from the Central Bank stating that it was a public office and the employees were public servants. In response to a question on this matter the Minster for Finance said,

> "The central bank is a statutory body; it was established in 1942 in accordance with the Central Bank Act 1942 and is now a constituted part of the European System of Central Banks (ESCB) established by the European Treaty. It is managed and controlled by the Central Bank Commission.....
> .....The Central Bank is independent in the exercise of its functions..."

So here is what we know. The banks that got Ireland in trouble, and that are being bailed out are owned by the government of Ireland. The Central Bank that governs these banks is run by a commission that is government appointed. That commission is headed by a governor who is ex-IMF and answerable to Minister for Finance who is the only shareholder in the Central Bank, even though the Central Bank is 'independent'. Furthermore, the Central Bank of Ireland is a stakeholder in the European Central Bank which is in business with the IMF and they make up two of the three parts of the Troika, the third being the EU Commission which ensures that the business of the European Union gets priority treatment above the business of individual countries. It appears that you are seen as nothing more than collateral damage. Welcome to the realisation that you do not matter.

Now we know that the entire system is one organisation with many faces and one agenda; to take control of the entire global finance system. This is not a conspiracy theory. There is no question that the world's finances are being driven by a small group of people who have learned how to create a monopoly, hide it behind smoke and mirrors, confuse it with figures and a language that few people understand. It is protected by a legal system that is also managed by the same people who run the money game. Currently the people of Ireland, along with those in many counties, are being duped into thinking that there is a recession as a result of a crisis within the banking world. The truth is that we are victims of the greed, control and desire for authority of just a few people who have carefully designed and methodically planned what we are currently experiencing.

'welcome to the realisation that you don't matter'

What are we experiencing?

Fear, confusion and the need for help! The old saying that a drowning man will grasp at a straw in the hope of getting above the surface is an apt description. The fear mongering game has done a clean sweep and the people of Ireland are now screaming for salvation. Nobody knows what to do, so they look to the bankers and government for leadership... while all the time we are being pulled further into the illusion. Most people have been so affected by their experiences that they have forgotten what matters most and what they are capable of.

I spoke to a 39 year old man last year who told me the story of his life as a teenager. In his mid teens he was groomed by a priest who was the principal of his school and who was a master of his trade (abuse not teaching). He knew what to say, how to say it and when to say it. He knew what to do, how to do it and when to do it. He also knew how to create a real and powerful fear in this young boy. Once he had the boy groomed and lost in the illusionary world he had created for him he sexually abused him, not once or twice but many times. The man often asked as he was processing his abuse with his therapist how it could happen again and again and why this man held so much power over him. He learned that life, the mind, heart, soul, and everyone's need to belong, succeed, be happy and feel purpose and meaning were very complex and powerful realities. He learned that the power of the abuser comes from the weakness, fear, guilt and responsibility that he carefully creates in the world of the one he is abusing.

Is this what the banks have been doing to us?

Yes, the banks and their government cronies have been grooming us. They know what to say, when to say it and how to say it. They also know what to do, when to do it and how to do it so that you feel:

Fearful
Guilty
Regretful
Panicked
Responsible
Lost
Helpless
Disempowered
Reliant
A Failure
Desperate to Fix what is Broken

Why has it not been stopped?

Who will stop it; the few trailblazers who are regularly ridiculed? Remember, the people are conditioned to believe what the banks and the governments want them to believe. They are afraid not to.

Many attempts were made to communicate with the Central Bank while this book was being written. On numerous occasions I contacted them with a number of questions, however, they simply refused to answer what I believed were legitimate and fair questions in relation to the banking system, the financial situation that Ireland found itself in and entanglements that are very clearly on show in respect to Ireland and Europe. In the following pages you can read a selection of emails that were sent to and received from the Central Bank of Ireland. As you look through these emails you will see a deliberate and unapologetic attempt to avoid interaction.

What do they have to hide?

Following these emails you can read the list of questions they refused to answer.

From: Marcus McKeown
Sent: 18 November 2011 16:32
To: Enquiries
Subject: questions
Importance: High

TO WHOM IT MAY CONCERN:

I would appreciate your answer to the following few question. I have read the Central Bank website in full and would ask that these questions are directly answered and I am not directed to aspects or elements of the website.

Can I please ask that you offer a response to these questions as soon as possible:

1. In relation to a loan (e.g. A mortgage) with a bank being securitized and sold in a bond:
    i. What is the name of the document that is used to record the transaction?
    ii. Who draws up/creates this document?
    iii. Who is responsible for keeping the document on file i.e. does the bank in question and the central bank both keep a copy of the document for their files or is it just one of the organisations that keep it on record?

2. In relation to tracing an individual loan that may have been securitized:
    i. What is the process used to trace an individual loan in order to discover if it has been securitized?
    ii. If a person is aware that their loan has been securitized what is the process of tracing that loan in order to discover what bond it was placed into?
3. In relation to securitized loans and bank balance sheets:
    i. In certain central bank spread sheets e.g. A.6. Loans to Irish Residence, the securitized loan balances are deducted from the bank's balance sheets. Can you confirm why these figures are deducted... is it because the loan has been settled by consequence of the securitization process and the monies received to purchase the bond? If not please explain the reason for the deductions.
4. Is the Central Bank privately owned or publically owned?
5. Who are the shareholders of the Central Bank of Ireland?
6. What other organisations have a stake in the Irish Central Bank?
7. What other organisations does the Irish Central Bank have a stake in?
8. Who owns the European Central Bank?
9. Who are the shareholders of the ECB and what are their positions do they hold in the bank or other organisations within or outside the finance world?
10. Who owns the World Bank?
11. Who are the shareholders of the World Bank and what are the positions they hold in the bank or other organisations within or outside the finance world?
12. Who owns the IMF?
13. Who are the shareholders of the IMF?
14. What is the BIS and what exactly is its role?
15. Who owns the BIS?
16. Is there any connection at a director level, board level or private investment level between the Federal Reserve in The USA and the Central Bank of Ireland, ECB, IMF and World Bank?

Marcus McKeown

From: [redacted]
Sent: 23 November 2011
To: Marcus McKeown
Subject: questions

Dear Mr. McKeown,

I refer to your emails of 18 and 21 November.

The website is the primary source of information produced by the Central Bank of Ireland for members of the public with technical queries and contains extensive information about financial regulation. I suggest you refer to the Financial Regulation section of the website for information about the authorisation and supervision requirements and processes.

In relation to questions 1-3 below, each borrower can request this information from the lending institution. I would refer you to our Annual Report where you will find replies to a number of the questions you ask about the Central Bank and governance. The Annual Report is available on the website but I will be happy to send you a hard copy if you send me a postal address. Alternatively you can pick up a copy from the Reception area of our Dame Street offices. Ex officio members of the Commission are members by virtue of the office they hold and have the exact same rights as other members including the same right to vote.

Central Bank employees are public servants.

As already advised on the phone, the Quarterly Financial Accounts data gives you the liabilities of the household sector in Ireland. If you wish to divide this by the population of Ireland, population data is available from the CSO.

http://www.centralbank.ie/polstats/stats/qfaccounts/Pages/Data.aspx

http://www.cso.ie/

As previously advised, mortgage data is available in Table A.6 of the Money and Banking statistics.

http://www.centralbank.ie/polstats/stats/cmab/Pages/Money%20and%20Banking.aspx

Please read both sets of explanatory notes, which explains the coverage of both sets of statistics.

We do not provide information about other organisations such as the ECB, BIS, IMF, World Bank etc. The information you require is publicly available or you might want to direct your questions to the relevant organisations.

It has come to my attention that you have been in contact with a number of different departments in the Central Bank. Please direct all future relevant requests for information that cannot be obtained on the website to the Public Contacts Unit at enquiries@centralbank.ie.

Yours sincerely,

Public Contacts Unit

From: Marcus McKeown
Sent: 18 November 2011 18:12
To:
Subject: questions
Importance: High

Dear

Thanks you for your reply, I appreciate you taking the time to send the same. However the email sent to you had a number of specific questions that it seems remain unanswered, the questions can once again be read by scrolling down on this email.

I would once again like to officially request that you, or the appropriate person in your office respond to these questions. I do not wish to be directed to your website as I have read in full the website and many of the documents embedded in the same. The questions are listed as I am seeking clarification after having read the website. They are very specific questions and I am requesting specific responses to the same.

It is my understanding that I am within my right to request specific answers to specific questions and the Central Bank should it choose to not offer those specific answers is in neglect of its duties. If you continue not to answer these questions I would ask that you respond with an explanation of why this is so.

Wishing you well,

Regards,

Marcus

From: Marcus McKeown
Sent: 18 November 2011 22:19
To: [redacted]
Subject: questions
Importance: High

Hi [redacted]

Along with the questions I have already email to you I have attached a document with a number of other questions that I would like to have addressed by the Central Bank. I would appreciate if the central bank would respond to each question with an actual answer. These are very specific questions and the answers are not available on the Central Banks website.

Should you have any questions or queries in relation to the same I would ask that you email or phone me (the number is given below). I would also that you email me with a full explanation if there is a problem with the Central Bank answering these questions or if it is not in a position to do so.

Thank you again for your help,

I look forward to hearing from you

Regards,

Marcus

From: [redacted]
Sent: 25 November 2011 16.43
To: Marcus McKeown
Subject: questions

Dear Mr. McKeown

I acknowledge receipt of your emails of 23 November 2011 in which you set out a substantial number of questions.

The Central Bank of Ireland has responsibility for the financial health and stability of the Irish financial services industry and combines the former roles of the Central Bank with previous prudential and conduct of business supervision responsibilities of the Financial Regulator.

All information in the public domain regarding Central Bank of Ireland activities and relevant surrounding legislation is outlined on our website for members of the public to access. We have already advised you of this.

The Central Bank of Ireland cannot comment on or answer questions about other organisations and you should direct your questions to the relevant organisations.

We cannot be of any further assistance to you and our correspondence on this matter is now closed.

Yours sincerely

[redacted]

Public Contacts Unit

From: Marcus McKeown
Sent: 28 November 2011 15:28
To: [redacted]
Subject: questions
Importance: High

Hi [redacted]

I was surprised to get your email stating that you were 'closing' the matter in relation to the questions I sent you. The questions are a part of legitimate research and I am confused as to who would give the order within the Central Bank to refuse to answer questions from the general public and from an Irish Person in particular. You stated in one of your emails to me that the employees of the central bank are public services workers which leads me to believe that the central bank is a publically owned organisation. Can you please write to inform me as to how your office, which is a public service office can refuse to respond to genuine questions from the public in relation to the business of the said office and organisation.

Can you also clarify for me who specifically you are referring to when you state that the 'Central Bank of Ireland cannot comment on or answer questions'. I am assuming that you have been instructed to offer me this information from another living person within the central bank as I am aware that the bank is a legal fiction and it itself can walk, talk, respond, instruct, give orders or offer answers, I am therefore assuming that one of two things has happened:

1. Another party instructed you to respond with a refusal to answer the questions placed before you or
2. You have taken upon yourself to speak on behalf of the Bank and refuse to offer the answers to the questions placed before you

Please advise me as to what exactly happened and if it was a person other than yourself that instructed the response I would ask that you let me know the name and rank of the said party.

I am once again making an official request that the questions sent to your office are answered and that each and every answer provided is both an honest and full response.

I am also happy to come into your office and sit with any and all persons required in order to have a conversation that will offer the answers being sought

Thank you for your time. In anticipation of a favourable reply,

Regards,

Marcus McKeown

From: [redacted]
Sent: 02 December 2011 10.39
To: Marcus McKeown
Subject: questions

Dear Mr. McKeown,

I note your comments and also note that you have submitted your list of questions as part of research which you are undertaking. The Central Bank of Ireland does not offer a research facility to members of the public. As I have already advised you, information on the Central Bank is available on our website. I cannot be of further assistance to you.

Yours sincerely,

Public Contacts Unit

The End

<u>The following is the list of questions sent to the Central Bank.</u>

1. With regard to the general question of the governance by the Central Bank of the Irish banks, can you please state:

a. How is the 'disappearance' of the billions of Euro, now being replaced by the billions that the Government decided to pay to the banks, explained and where have those billions 'gone'?
b. Where is the money that is now being given to banks coming from?
c. How much money precisely has been given or will be given to each of the Irish banks by the Government in the context of the so-called 'bail-out'?
d. Who precisely made the decision to grant those monies and has the Central Bank a recommendatory role in that regard?
e. Is it a condition of the money being given to the banks that it be used by for express and exact purposes, such as clearing bank debt, as working capital, or for some other specific purposes, or is it entirely a matter for the banks themselves as to how they use the 'bail-out' funds? Does the Central Bank have governance role in that regard?
f. If so, how is that monitoring process undertaken?
g. Is there any upper limit to the amounts being given to each bank and does the Central Bank have any role in that regard?
h. Are there any conditions whatsoever attaching to the monies being given by the Government to the banks and is the Central Bank monitoring the observance of any such conditions?
i. If such conditions exist, what are they?

j. Is the observance of any such conditions being independently monitored?

2. With regard to the guarantees given to the Irish banks by the Government in September 2008, please outline any role undertaken by the Central Bank or any officer of the Bank in relation to them.

3. With regard to the Central Bank of Ireland, please state:

a. Who owns the Central Bank? Is it State-owned, privately-owned or a combination of both?
b. What are the names and details of the directors and principal shareholders of the Central Bank of Ireland, whether privately-owned or otherwise?
c. Who appoints the shareholders and directors?
d. If owned and operated on behalf of the State, who actually carries out this remit, how are such directors and shareholders appointed, and to whom and in what manner are they accountable?

4. With regard to the private commercial banks operating in Ireland which have benefitted from a subvention from the Government, is the Central Bank fully aware of and in possession of the following data:The names and other relevant data of the directors of each?

a. The names and other relevant data relating to the so-called 'public interest' directors on the bank boards in Ireland?
b. In what way is the remit of the 'public interest' directors different to that of other directors of those

banks and is there any interaction between them and the Central Bank of Ireland?

c. Do these latter issue publicly-available reports on their performance or general stewardship?
d. Is a copy of the written conditions of employment and contractual obligations applicable to 'public interest directors' publicly available?

5. With regard to the general question of the Central Bank's bank regulation of banks in Ireland, please state:

a. Who is responsible for ensuring compliance with the statutory and code-of-practice regulation of banks and other financial institutions generally in the State?
b. In the event that the Central Bank of Ireland was doing its statutory functions in relation to its supervisory role of the banks in Ireland correctly and to the highest standards, how was it possible for the Irish banks to effectively collapse and become insolvent?
c. Does the Governor of the Central Bank and Financial Regulator have written contracts of employment with clear performance-related conditions?
d. In the context of the performance of their duties by the Governor of the Central Bank and the Financial Regulator, is a code of practice, or code of conduct, an integral element of their employment contracts and conditions?
e. Did the immediately-preceding Financial Regulators and Governors of the Central Bank of Ireland have written contracts of employment?
f. In the view of the Central Bank of Ireland and in the light of the collapse of the banking system and the

consequent 'bail-out' by the government, and the prior assurances given by the then Financial Regulator and Central Bank Governor to the contrary, did the lack of performance of these two most recent holders of the offices of Governor of the Central Bank and Financial Regulator raise questions about the degree to which they honoured those contracts?

g. What if any is the significance of the recent amendment to advertising code practice that states that regulation is now implemented by "the Central Bank of Ireland" as opposed to "the Financial Regulator," which assertion was in place until recently.

6. With regard to the definition of a bank, can you please state:

a. What is the legal definition of a 'bank' in Ireland?
b. What is the legal definition of a 'banker' and may a 'banker' lawfully be an individual?

7. Is the Central Bank of Ireland responsible for the issuance of the Irish Euro currency, and what are the applicable criteria for such issuance?

8. With regard to the creation of the Irish Euro, please state:

a. Is this money created electronically 'from fresh air,' without relationship to underlying assets?
b. If not, what assets underpin the creation of Irish bank notes?

c. Does the Central Bank insist that loans advanced by banks should be underpinned by assets or deposits of any kind held by those issuing banks?
d. Who decides what quantities of the Irish Euro are printed?
e. How often is the printing of such notes undertaken, in what quantities and at whose instruction?
f. Is the Irish Euro note printed in Ireland? If not, where?
g. How is that printing process monitored and by whom?
h. Is such money generation generally carried out as a short or long-term liquidity measure as in, say, an asset purchase facility fund, or for the purposes of so-called 'quantitative easing' to facilitate banks within the State, or in response to some other requirement or stated criteria, or under what other conditions?

9. With regard to the general question of bank licences necessary to operate in Ireland, please state:

a. Can the Central Bank of Ireland make available copies of the licences and licence conditions issued to each of the banks operating in Ireland?
b. If not, where are copies of the licences and licence conditions under which each of our banks function available?
c. Are the licence conditions governing 'foreign' banks operating in Ireland different in any way to those of the so-called 'Irish' banks?
d. Is it possible in any circumstances to trade as a bank in Ireland without a licence?
e. Who is responsible for monitoring banks' compliance with the conditions of their banking licences?

f. Is compliance by the banks with their licence conditions transparent, how is this demonstrated and does the Central Bank have a role in this regard?
g. What action does the Central Bank take, and what is the Central Bank's view, about the legal consequences arising for banks and their customers if such banks have breached one or more of the conditions of their banking licences?
h. In the view of the Central Bank, if a bank has been operating in breach of one or more of conditions of their licence, are the Agreements they have entered into while so doing legally binding?
i. If a bank is offering and selling loans and mortgages while insolvent, is it in breach of the conditions of its licence to operate as laid down by the Central Bank or otherwise?
j. When was the last review of licence conditions governing financial institutions and who is responsible for such reviews?

10. With regard to the concept of fractional reserve banking, or fractional reserve lending, please outline the Central Bank's view and the statutory situation in relation to each of the following:

a. What precise criteria in relation to fractional reserve banking, if any, apply to the banks in the context of their lending policies?
b. Are banks obliged to retain at least certain minima of retained deposits relative to their lending volumes, and if so, what are these ratios, and how does the Central Bank monitor such compliance?

c. What minima of liquid cash reserves, or liquidity ratios, are financial institutions obliged to retain in their reserves at all times?
d. Who decides what the ratios relating to solvency and liquidity should be?
e. Who monitors compliance with any such strictures, and how?
f. Are such ratios arbitrary or are they governed by statute or otherwise?
g. What changes in these regulations have there been over the years?
h. By what mechanism can an insolvent bank give out loans or offer mortgages if it is 'broke' and has no money?

11. With regard to mortgages and other loans advanced by banks under the licences issued by the Central Bank, can you please clarify:

a. What is the precise mechanism and procedure by which such banks extend 'loans' and 'facilities' to clients?
b. What the process is by which banks raise the monies they loan out and where does that money come from?
c. Is it true to say that, typically, a bank seeks firstly to secure the written undertaking of a would-be borrower to repay a loan over a number of years and then uses that pledge or 'promissory note' to raise the necessary finance from other institutions or individuals by pledging or selling-on the document that the would-be borrower has signed?

d. Is it standard or common practice for banks to sell or trade onwards the 'agreements' they have put in place with their borrowers?
e. If that is so, is it also a fair statement to say that when the borrower signs the document agreeing to repay, he or she has effectively 'created' the basis for the generation of the money?
f. Is it the case that the signed agreements to repay over lengthy periods, as signed by the typical borrower, are typically 'sold on' in effect by the lending institution in order to raise the necessary line of credit from which the proposed loan will come?

12. With regard to the funding that the Government secured from Europe for the recapitalisation of Irish banks and other purposes, please state:

a. What role did or does the Central Bank have in that whole process?
b. Who or what organisation gave this so-called European 'bailout' money to Ireland to assist the maintenance of its solvency?
c. Is the disbursement of such monies undertaken by the Central Bank of Ireland or otherwise?
d. Are the European entities that gave this 'bailout' money to Ireland privately-owned, publicly-owned, State-owned, owned by a number of States, or owned by some other conglomeration?
e. Who sits on the boards, and who are the shareholders, of the organisation(s) in question?
f. Who precisely makes decisions to turn on or off the funding 'tap' in relation to the supply of ongoing

funding to Ireland in the event that such a decision was to be made? Is any such decision a political or an internal administrative decision?

g. Who and by what process was the 'troika' that are approving or otherwise of Ireland's adherence to the European funding Agreement appointed and to whom are they answerable? Does the Central Bank of Ireland have any interaction with the 'troika'?

13. With regard to the solvency of banks and recent so-called 'stress tests,' that were applied to the banks in Ireland, please state:

a. What was the specific assessment of how well each of the banks operating in Ireland is complying with solvency and liquidity requirements and what were the specific criteria assessed in relation to the Irish banks?
b. Who carried out these tests and what was the cost of same?

14. With regard to the nature of money and the money system that operates under the aegis of the Central Bank of Ireland, please clarify:

a. What is the correct legal, lawful or commercial name(s) ascribed to the following: cash, cheque, promissory note, IOU, electronic funds? Are these items deemed to be legal tender, lawful tender, lawful money, legal currency, or do they have some other 'title'?
b. What exactly is 'money of exchange'?
c. What exactly is 'money of account'?

d. What are the legal and other distinctions between money of exchange (presumably cash in hand supported by real assets) and money of account (presumably unsupported and without assets backing it up)?
e. Is it an accurate characterisation to say that banks typically advance a borrower 'money of account' while seeking repayment from borrowers by 'money of exchange'?

15. With regard to a borrower's agreeing to repay bank borrowings, please state:

a. Is it correct to say that in agreements between banks and borrowers, the promise to pay is the essential asset in the transaction?
b. If a bank creates a credit line on the back of the borrower's signature, and the consequent mortgage thus becomes an asset of the bank, in what way does that 'asset' continue to constitute a 'debt'?

16. In relation to the selling on by banks of loans, mortgages and other borrowings, and the governance of such transactions under the aegis of the Central Bank of Ireland, can you please state:

a. What are the legal requirements governing the selling-on by financial institutions to others of the loans they have advanced to borrowers for mortgages, property, etc?
b. What statutes govern the selling of loans and debt in Ireland?

c. If a debt is 'sold on,' is it accurate to say that the 'original' indebtedness has been technically cleared, that the original debt has thus been repaid to the original lender, and that as a consequence no direct contract exists between the borrower and the new purchasing 'owner'?
d. Is it lawful for a financial institution to 'sell-on' a debt without full prior disclosure to the borrower, thus binding the borrower to a new contracted party and potentially changing the conditions of the 'loan' in so doing?
e. Are there any particular standards of compliance or necessary conditions governing the selling-on of loans by foreign financial institutions operating in Ireland?

17. With regard to the sale of mortgages, can you please state:

    a. When a mortgage is securitised and sold to the market, is it sold as a 'security'?
    b. If so, does the instrument remain a 'mortgage' following the sale?
    c. If it is no longer a mortgage, can it ever again become a mortgage?
    d. If it is true that the Irish banks prepare and submit 'promissory notes' to the Central Bank as mortgaged-backed debt instruments, from what documents do these 'promissory notes' arise or on what are they based?
    e. Are those primary documents mortgage deeds? Or are they facility or offer letters, or some other type of instrument or document?

18. With regard to the presentation and depiction of various assets and liabilities in bank statements in the banks licensed and regulated by the Central Bank of Ireland, please state:

a. What particular minimal requirements does the Central Bank insist on in relation to the presentation of accounts and audited returns from the banks which it has licensed and which it regulates?
b. When a mortgage is logged as an asset in such banks, does that bank also open a liability account in respect of the same mortgage? What are the implications of that provision?
c. What is the purpose of opening the asset book and the liability book in respect of the same transaction?
d. Is a bank statement to a borrower a full and true account of the bank's affairs with that borrower, or does the statement represent only a *part* of the bank's account, namely the bank's depiction of one part of the equation relating to their business with their client?
e. If a bank is asked to verify a claim of injury by presenting their accounts when a person does not repay a loan, do those accounts show an actual loss for the bank in relation to that individual?
f. Is it the practice for the bank to lodge all account information into one 'client account', or does it keep individual and separate accounts in relation to that client, and has the Central Bank any particular requirements in that regard?
g. When a mortgage is taken out by a lender it is lodged into the banks 'asset book.' What exactly is the specific 'asset' that the bank is logging as theirs? Is it

the mortgaged property, the loan itself, the borrower's signature and related 'promissory note,' or something else?

h. What is the name given to the document that is created and used to record the sale of a bank asset? Who prepares the document? Where is it stored and what information does it contain?

19. In relation to the taking out of default insurance by banks, please state:

a. Is the taking out of such insurance a condition laid down by the Central Bank of Ireland?
b. Is it normal practice for banks to take out default insurance on loans?
c. Is there a legal regulation or any other rule of enforcement stating that a bank must insure its loans against default?
d. If yes, with whom is this insurance policy placed?
e. Is there any legal regulation applicable to financial institutions and banks obliging them to retain a provision fund or deposit account to clear defaulted loans?
f. If yes, what is the regulation? If no, is it nonetheless common practice for banks to set up such accounts in order to offset defaulted loans?
g. What is the time limit within which a bank must clear defaulted loan accounts?

20. What regulations or conditions are applied by the Central Bank of Ireland to protect the deposits of customers of

financial institutions and what sanctions are in place to deal with abuses of any such regulations or conditions?

21. In the context of borrower-bank transactions, what is the view of the Central Banks in relation to the view that, as taxpayers now 'own' large percentages of various banks by virtue of very large publicly subscribed recapitalisation, some element of the individual taxpayer's contribution to the 'bail-out' of a bank should be offset against any monies allegedly owed by that individual to such a bank?

22. What safeguards are in place to prevent a possible conflict of interest in relation to the European Central Bank's insistence that the Government pays off the Anglo-Irish bond-holders, in the context where the names of the benefitting bond-holders are being denied to the Government and the Central Bank of Ireland and the Government cannot therefore guarantee that there is no relationship between the members of the Board of the ECB who are enforcing this insistence on bondholder payouts, and the benefitting bondholders?

23. Is it ever the case that public servants leaving the employment of the Central Bank, the Financial Regulator's office, or the Department of Finance are subsequently employed, directly or indirectly, in any capacity by banks and are there any restrictions in place to avoid the possibility of conflict of interest in such a context?

24. In relation to the European Central Bank, please state:

    a. What is the relationship between the Central Bank of Ireland and The European Central Bank?
    b. Who owns the European Central Bank and who are its directors and shareholders?
    c. Is the European Central Bank connected in any way to any other national Central Bank?

25. In relation to the International Monetary Fund, please state:

    a. What is the relationship, if any, between the Central Bank of Ireland and the International Monetary Fund?
    b. Who owns the International Monetary Fund and who are its directors and shareholders?
    c. Is the International Monetary Fund connected in any way to any other Central Bank or any other monetary fund?

26. In what way, if any, are the European Central Bank and the International Monetary Fund connected to the American Federal Reserve?

27. Is the Central Bank of Ireland a member of, or connected in any way to, to the Irish Banking Federation?

    a. Does the Irish Banking Federation have any formal or other role in licensing of domestic or international banks in Ireland?

b. What is the nature of the relationship, if any, between the Irish Banking Federation and the Central Bank of Ireland?

28. In relation to money in circulation in Ireland, please state:

a. In the following years, what was the amount of currency in circulation in Ireland: 1990, 1995, 2000, 2003, 2004, 2005, 2006, 2007, 2008, 2009, 2010 and 2011?
b. In relation to the years that show a significant increase where did this money come from in each such year?
c. Who made the decision, and what was the mechanism for making such decision, in relation to controlling the increase or decrease in supply in those years?

29. With further regard to the Central Bank of Ireland, can you please say:

a. What is the total number of staff employed by the Central Bank of Ireland?
b. What is the total annual payroll of the Central Bank of Ireland?

Ends

A number of attempts were also made to get the Department of Finance to respond to the same questions. But no surprise in hearing that I received four read receipts following my email being sent but I am still waiting for a reply. Finally I received an email informing me that they would not answer the questions, I wonder why?

Chapter 8

The Answer Is In The Question

Did You Know

- If you ask powerful questions you will get powerful answers.
- The answer is in the question and knowing what to ask will set you free.
- The banking system is built on contradictions and the banks hope that you will get lost in the layers of confusion that will stop you asking the questions that will uncover their deceit

Everything I am hearing makes sense. I see the game being played out by the banking world and I accept that the system is doing what it needs to do in order to maintain control, but what can I do to expose the bankers so that I can get back to normal?

For most people asking the questions that will make a difference can be difficult as they do not understand the banking and money game enough to know what to ask. Perhaps the following questions will help to understand what is happening when you enter into a loan agreement with a bank.

1. Does the borrower or the bank legally own the promissory note?

   If they say that you own the promissory note, they are saying that it is yours and they cannot use it for their benefit. However, if they say that they own it then they must show what consideration was agreed in order for this to be so. There must be some consideration i.e. something given to the borrower in order for the bank to own it. The question is, what consideration was given?

2. Was the bank loan cheque or another similar instrument the consideration that the bank loaned in order for it to legally own the promissory note?

   If the bank says that it was not the cheque or another financial instrument, they are stating that they gave nothing to own the note. If they say that it was the cheque (or another instrument) they are saying that the note funded the cheque and they must once again prove that this was legal and that both parties in the transaction were aware of what and why it was happening. There must also be full disclosure in relation to the legal implications of this happening.

3. Is a cheque considered money or just an order to pay money?
   If they say that it is money, this means that you can write a cheque to clear your alleged debt without having to put money into the account and the cheque will be accepted as money. In which case, they will tell you that the cheque is an order to pay only.

4. Does the bank policy prevent the borrower from clearing a debt with the same kind of funds used to issue the loan cheque?
   If they answer to the affirmative, they are agreeing that they are simply money changers and they loaned no valuable consideration to own the promissory note. However, if they say 'no' and agree that the borrower can clear the alleged debt with the same kind of funds as originally provided by the bank, they must accept from the borrower a second promissory note to discharge the original note. The borrower can then issue a promissory note with no interest or loan agreement. If they do not answer they are showing that there is no mutual understanding in the agreement and the agreement is void.

5. Is the borrower's promissory note the same as cash or actual cash according to the banking policy?
   It does not matter what they say here because the important thing is the bank's intent. If they claim that the promissory note was the same as cash or was actual cash, they are saying that the borrower gave cash or the equivalent to fund the loan cheque. Of course, if the borrower gave cash to fund the cheque then the borrower owes nothing, for how could he? In this case, it was an exchange and not a loan.

6. Do you understand that the borrower gave the bank permission to sell the promissory note and use the proceeds to fund the bank loan cheque to the borrower?
   If you are told this is the case then the bank are agreeing that they loaned nothing to own the promissory note and they received something of value from the borrower for free, sold it and returned the proceeds back to the borrower. This will help in the process of beginning to understand who funded the cheque that was given to the borrower. If the borrower funded the cheque via his promissory note he cannot owe the bank anything.

7. Is your understanding of the intent behind the agreement, that the party who provided the capital for the original alleged loan cheque is repaid in full the amount of the capital used to fund the cheque?
   If they say 'yes' then the next question is clear.

8. Who funded the capital for the original loan cheque? If they say that it was they who funded the cheque, they must prove how they funded the capital for the cheque. Remember, they did not have the money to fund the cheque so they cannot prove they funded it without lying and misleading you. If they say they did not fund the cheque then you want to know who did and they must show you all the documents that support their claim.

9. According to your understanding of the alleged agreement, was the borrower to loan or give the lender something of value before the bank granted the alleged borrower a bank loan?
   If you are told 'yes' then the bank is admitting that they loaned nothing of value to obtain the promissory note and the money to fund the cheque came from the borrower. If the bank does not answer this question then there is no understanding of the agreement and therefore no agreement exists.

10. According to the loan agreement, explain the paper trail and forensic reality in relation to the banks book keeping entries between the borrower and the lender in order for the bank to own the promissory note.

11. Identify where within all the terms and agreements of the loan does the bank explain in full the facts concerning the money trail and what the lender is required to do in order to own the promissory note.

12. Is it legal and lawful for the bank to accept funds from the customer, deposit these funds and write a cheque from these funds without the customer's express written permission, knowledge and understanding? Please provide the paperwork that shows this.

13. Did the borrower give the bank authorisation to receive funds from the borrower and use the funds to issue a cheque back to the same customer and call it a bank loan?

14. According to Irish and European bank policy and procedures and standard book keeping entries, who loaned what to whom. Be specific?

15. According to banking policy, do the banks' debts increase when the bank issues a loan?

16. Does a cheque transfer a bank liability from one chequeing account to another?

17. According to banking policy what exact species of money was the borrower to repay the bank debt with?

18. According to banking policy what are the species of money that a borrower can use to repay a debt?

19. Is a cheque considered cash or a promise to pay?

20. What species of money was used to fund the original loan cheque?

21. For a cheque to be valid, must cash or something that has actual cash value first be deposited to fund the cheque? Are there ever any exceptions to this and if so what are they?

22. Does your bank have cash money in reserve to cover all its lending?

23. If your bank does not have actual cash money to cover all its lending what does it lend out to the borrower?

24. What is 'money' according to banking policy and procedures?

25. Is the bank policy to put a stamp, writing or any other mark on the promissory note after the borrower has signed it? If so what is the stamp, mark or writing that is placed on the note and by whom is it placed there?

26. What is the meaning and purpose of stamping the note 'pay to the order of'?

27. Would the transaction change if the stamp, writing or mark was not placed on the note?

28. Is a copy of the promissory note with the new mark, stamp or writing upon it given to the customer after the mark is placed there?

29. Is it bank policy to inform the customer that the promissory note will be altered in any way after they have signed it?

30. What are the financial regulations in relation to informing the customer of alterations to their promissory note after they have signed it?

31. What is your bank's 'in house' policy in relation to informing customers of alterations to the promissory note after the customer has signed it?

32. If the bank receives money from the Central Bank, do the bank's assets and liabilities increase? Explain in detail what happens in this case and why?

33. Does the word 'loan' mean that it is a loan according to the banking policy, practise or procedure? If the answer is 'no' then explain what 'loan' means, and if the answer is 'yes' please provide the exact definition according to your policy and procedures of the word "loan"?

34. Does the word 'borrower' mean a borrower or is there another meaning in the banking world for this word?

35. Does ‘interest’ mean the charge applied for the use of borrowed money?

36. According to your interpretation of the agreement, does the bank loan a cheque to the borrower in order for the bank to legally own the promissory note or does the borrower give the bank the promissory note for free and then the bank returns the value of the promissory note to the borrower as a loan?

37. According to your understanding, does the bank legally own the promissory note without loaning the borrower a cheque or other instrument, or must the bank first loan the borrower a cheque or similar instrument in order for the bank to legally own the promissory note?

38. Do you believe that the bank owned the promissory note before or after the bank issued the loan cheque?

39. From your experience, understanding and knowledge of the banking world, when a bank records new deposits and liabilities, does it mean that the bank received money from a banking customer? Are there any exceptions to this?

40. Do you believe that the alleged borrower agreed to bring a promissory note to the bank to create a new deposit, then the bank issued a cheque from a new

deposit and returned the cheque back to the same alleged depositor or borrower or seller of the property and that the cheque is called a loan? If this is so, where is this information provided in writing?

41. If a bank receives cash money from a customer and that is deposited thereby creating a new deposit, would the bank then owe that customer that amount of cash? If the customer deposited a cheque or promissory note into a chequeing account would the bank owe that customer money?

42. Does a deposit mean that the bank owes money?

43. According to your understanding, did the bank use the promissory note to create a new deposit on the bank's books? Does the bank owe somebody money for this new deposit and if so, who?

44. Do you believe that the alleged borrower intended for his promissory note be used to fund his loan?

45. Is there a policy, procedure or regulation that requires those selling loans or other finance products to have passed exams? If so, what are the exams and who is the governing body in relation to them?

46. Had the person who signed off the loan passed their exams at the time of signing?

47. Is there a legal requirement or a bank policy that requires the bank representative to ensure that the customer is fully clear in his understanding of what is happening, the intent behind what is happening and the consequences?

48. Can a bank write a cheque without first depositing money?

49. When the bank grants loans, do banks receive an asset from the borrower which results in a new deposit?

50. Does the bank write a cheque from a new deposit and call this a loan to the borrower?

51. Is recording a new deposit a loan? If no, explain what recording a new deposit is?

52. Is a bank loan a bank transaction of receiving funds and issuing a cheque against those funds?

53. Does the bank receive funds from the customer for free?

54. How much money did the bank risk or loan in order to obtain the promissory note?

55. Is the original promissory note a negotiable instrument, commercial paper or Money?

56. Do you have any knowledge of a bank using a promissory note without altering it to fund a bank loan or cheque?

57. If a customer deposits cash into an account, do the bank assets and liabilities increase?

58. Does the bank liability indicate that the bank owes the depositor the value of the deposit?

59. Does the bank need available cash to pay its liability?

60. From an economic perspective, does a bank liability show the cash was loaned to the bank?

61. From an economic perspective, does a bank liability show that the bank owe money to the other party involved in the transaction? If not, explain.

62. Did the bank customer, investor or other depositor or someone else deposit the money used to fund the loan cheque in advance of it being issued?

63. Can the bank issue a cheque without first depositing money into the account from which the cheque is to be drawn?

64. If the bank does not deposit funds to issue cheques, then what does the bank call it if they receive funds from a customer that are used to fund the cheque?

65. Is a customer's promissory note a negotiable or commercial paper traded like money?

66. Does the bank accept anything other than cheques, drafts, cash and coins as money deposited to issue cheque based money?

67. Is the bank policy to claim a promise to pay the equivalent of actual money?

68. When a customer makes a deposit into the bank is that deposit recorded as an asset, a liability or both?

69. Does the bank deposit any funds that are not legal tender in order to create chequebook money?

70. Did the bank disclose all terms of the transaction in advance of the borrower signing the agreement or promissory note?

71. Do you believe beyond all doubt that your banks' customers who entered into alleged borrowing agreements with the bank were fully aware every aspect of the agreement they were entering into?

72. Do you believe that your banking customers who entered into alleged borrowing agreements with the bank were aware of every aspect of the bank's business with the customer's promissory note and

what was happening in relation to the same once the customer has signed the same?

73. Is credit the same as money?

74. Is credit the opposite of money?

I can see that these questions will compel the bank to give all of the information that the customer needs to understand what is happening within the banking system, but what specifically will they prove?
The answers to these questions will disclose the true intent behind the business of the bank in relation to lending. They will show that:

a. The intention is that the person or party who funded the capital for the loan should be repaid the amount they funded.
b. The borrower funded the loan.
c. Money is created from thin air.
d. The bank claimed ownership over the borrower's promissory note and gave no consideration for the same, which means the bank took for free the borrower's promissory note and then used it to fund the loan that the borrower was seeking.
e. It was the borrower who loaned the bank the money that the bank gave back to the borrower as a loan.
f. The bank lied to, misled and cheated the customer.

g. The banks are not banks in the context of what we have been educated to believe. They are only money changers.
h. The borrower owes the bank nothing.

Chapter 9

How Do The Banks Function?

Did You Know

- The illusion of money prevents you from remembering that you do not need money in order to have what you want and to live a happy life.
- As soon as everyone says 'give me my money' the banking system will fail because they have no money. It is the people who have money and the bank's success depends on us thinking that it is their money.
- The banks make you think they are smart by convincing you that you are stupid.

So the bank makes money if I do not know about the true nature of how they work. If I do not understand the bookkeeping part, I repay them the loan (that never existed) and that is how they profit, right?

That is only the start of what happens. The banks make money in many ways from your promissory note. Essentially the banks make money out of thin air! For most of my life I believed that something was happening at a deeper level that created life but I could not put my finger on it. I asked questions, like, why do we call glass, glass and not something else? Why do we call a jug a jug and not something else? The questions persisted until I realised that things are what they are because we make them so, we create them that way, we give them names, meaning and purpose and live as though there is no alternative. Similar questions occurred to me in relation to money like what is money? What gives it its value? Where did it come from? Why do we need it? Who gives it value? But most of all, how is money made? The answer is that money is made from thin air. It comes from nothing and in most cases the money that is made never truly exists and thanks to the world to technology it is easier than ever to make money without having to actually make money.

'The bank makes money out of thin air'

When I speak of money I refer to the illusion of money, because money is not real in the context that we have been educated. Once you understand this you will see many other things as a natural consequence of your new knowledge, understanding and wisdom.

The people behind the bank, let us call them the true bankers have the authority to create money because we give it to them. The fact that we allow it, allows it. From here the true bankers just need a system, a formula, a rule book and game plan in order to begin creating. Of course, if they just made money without some kind of illusionary system supporting what they do, we would realise that we could make money too and they would no longer be able to perform their magic. Consider it this way:

The game plan: get those who have money to give it to us and we will mind it for them and pay them a commission (interest). Now everyone thinks we have plenty of money and we are in a position to loan them what they need, which we do plus an interest charge. The assumption is that enough money is being printed and there is always enough money in the vault for us to have what we want in accordance with what we can pay back.

What happens next is the same trickery that has caused all the trouble. The banks, in partnership with governments and corporate organisations enter into the same game that the customer has started playing. They loan money to each other at a cost only, unlike the costumer, they cannot get into trouble because they can push the 'print it' button and make as much money as they need.

All this time the general public never realise that most of the money being spent is in electronic format. Maybe as little as three or four per cent of that exists, yet business continues as if there is a whole lot more.

So how do they do it?

For every amount of money taken in, the same amount is lent out ten times over. However, the amount we borrow (allegedly) is what they use to create the illusion of assets that support lending. It is no coincidence that if a bank claims to have made one hundred million profit in one year, their loan book will have increased by the same amount in the same year.

How?

Your promissory note is lodged into the bank's asset book and gives the bank the stated value. If a loan of €300,000.00 is considered an asset to the bank then the bank can lend up to ten times that much, and in some cases a lot more than that to their customers. This is known as fractional reserve banking.

But how can it lend €3,000,000.00 if it only has €300,000.00?

Stop assuming that money equals cash. It takes many forms. The bank can do this because they wrote the rules, manage the details of the accounts and keep the right people on the pitch. It is called 'fractional reserve banking' where they can lend out ten times, or more, the initial amount minus the percentage they must keep on reserve. So with a reserve requirement of 10% the bank lends out the other 90%, and the game goes on and before you know it, the initial three hundred thousand has developed into tens of millions (and maybe more) but all that must exist in cash is 10%. And even though that was the guideline many banks didn't even have that cash reserve available to them. Don't forget that banks are insolvent and have been for a very long time. They simply managed to get away with their illegal trading as long as they could keep the illusion alive. Even now with the illusion bust they are still trading illegally and they continue to keep the people in the dark as to their true state of being.

It is now clear that the banks have created the money out of thin air and we are only spending money that exists on a screen. Furthermore, the banks put their own illusionary money into investments for which they borrow from themselves and each other, and in creating this lending they are also creating more money, more lending power and more reserves to lend even more money. The figures eventually reach levels that go beyond comprehension. Now calculate the real value after the banks buy and sell their bonds, get paid on their loans plus the interest and the penalties as well as the charges. The numbers are staggering. All this electronic money is known as FIAT money. FIAT money is not real, it does not exist and your remaining ignorant to that fact is what allows the game to continue.

What happens when they have loaned everybody money?
They lend more. Remember the more they lend the more they can lend and the more they can lend the more their profits increase.

What happens after everybody has their loan and they have bought their house?
They are encouraged to buy another home. Because there is so much 'money' around (called free money) there are plenty of jobs and people can command good salaries with which they can manage their mortgage. However, at this stage of the game they have become dependent upon the illusion, are fearful of losing it and dismissive of anyone who suggests that it might end up being dropped into the psychological equivalent of Room 101. All this time you think you owned your new life but the truth is that the bank now owns you!

Does this apply to everyone?
Yes. The banks are in the business of making money and to do this they create assets, of which they need to give the impression that they are lending, and they will lend to anyone, even people with poor credit ratings.

Does this only apply to mortgages?
No, this is true for all lending; mortgages, credit cards, personal loans, overdrafts, car loans, home improvement loans and any other type of loan. Behind the scenes all

lending follows the same game plan as any other kind of lending.

So why are the banks in so much trouble at the moment?

They are not. The function of the bank is to make money and the bank makes money no matter what is happening in the market. The only thing that changes is how they make their money, the rate they make it and the way they can or cannot cover up what they are doing.

Take David for example, who owed €175,000.00 for a commercial property. After paying over €20,000.00 in interest only payments he still owed the full amount. The bank repossessed the property sold it for €60,000.00 and took him to court for the balance. On top of that they got a tax right off on the defaulted loan and it has been suggested that the bad debt was also protected by an insurance policy. Coupled with which, the bank also made money by lending money on the back of the original asset that David's loan created. That €175,000.00 loan created ten times that in lending for the bank plus the money made on the back of lending on the new loans (assets) created. The bank never loses because they are experts in the field, but that is all about to change.

How did this all begin and where did the first money come from?

Long ago people traded with the barter system. They swapped things they needed with things the other person needed. The barter worked well although there were obvious limits and issues. Precious metals, like gold were recognised as a way forward, and the goldsmiths of the time began to create small coins out of pure gold. These gold coins were used as a trading currency because it was easier to manage and enter into an exchange with something that everyone was accept as valuable.

Now somewhere was needed to store the coins, so the goldsmiths started to hold them on account, in exchange for a small fee. When someone wanted his gold coins he would go to the goldsmith who gave him his gold and take note of the transaction in his book (ledger). Soon the goldsmith realised that it was easier to keep the gold coins in a safe place and give a paper receipt (promissory notes) for each coin which can be used to trade.

After some time the goldsmith realised that his customers were happy to leave their gold coins on account, and seeing that few were bothered to withdraw them, he created more paper promissory notes that would be lent out with an interest charge, with the result that soon there were more promissory notes than gold coins. This was the beginning of paper money and as long as no one came looking to exchange their promissory notes for money the goldsmith could continue making interest on the back of gold he did not have.

This is like the current system. The banks lend out credit which is money they do not have and as long as everybody does not come looking for their money

at the same time the game continues and no one is any the wiser.
That is right, as long as the goldsmith was creating promissory notes, the value of goods was increasing as money became more plentiful. The result of which is inflation where the worker has to earn more money that is worth less. At this point you return to the goldsmith and take out a loan of some more promissory notes at an interest rate that pays him his profit. Now you are stuck in his game of life and he owns you.

So we create the new money that the banks use as assets, which in turn become the security that is used to stay in the game of lending and all this time we really owe them nothing because the true nature of what happens is an exchange of loans, and the debts are settled, is that right?
Yes.

Is there any good news at all?
You do not owe the banks any money

Yes, but this new information is having a hard time running the old beliefs out.
So, as you are in the middle of letting in some new information, would you like distraction for a while?

Is it going to upset me?
I don't think so.

Okay so...

We now know that your promissory note was lodged in the bank as an asset and that created new money. However the banks lied, misinformed you and by withholding the truth they were free to make you pay off the loan that you never really got as the money you "borrowed" was yours to begin with, right!

Yes, I've got that bit...

That means that the payments you have made to date on the loan you never got where payments you never really had to make. This would make these payments 'extortion', and by extortion I mean that the bank obtained money and or property illegally by the misuse of their position and power. The same logic would tell us that you are entitled to a refund for all those payments.

"Wow, I never thought of that but it makes perfect sense"

Applying the same logic we could also suggest that you are well and truly entitled to some if not all the proceeds from the profits that the bank made on the back of them selling your promissory note without your permission and without you fully understanding or knowing what the true intention behind the original transaction was.

You see, once you break through the smoke and mirrors, you can see right through the system.

What do you mean by smoke and mirrors?

This is a term that describes the distractions that are used in order to give the impression that what is happening is above board. In other words, the banks are projecting a particular situation as being truthful when something else is happening behind the scenes, like a fog that they create to prevent you seeing beyond a certain point.

The smoke and mirrors of language: the banks work with a different language by using words in a certain way and with a certain tone, pitch and emphasis that leaves the non-banker unsure of what is being said. They also use the said system to communicate internally and in doing that the front of house staff as kept just as ignorant as the general customer in terms of getting a true handle on how they work and what they are up to.

The smoke and mirrors of figure and formulas: the banks use figures and formulas that no one without expert training could understand. For the rest of us would be like trying to count the stars in the night sky. That is a certain number of stars up there and you know how to count but you just keep getting lost in the moving reality and distracted by the illusions of perception, not to mention that, all you can see does not necessarily equal all that is there. In relation to numbers and figures the banks make their greatest gain from what appears almost irrelevant... that is you and I! Here is an example of how playing with small numbers can give the impression of what is happening.

Paul goes to play golf with Mary and Mary says to Paul "let's play for a small wager, like 10cent per hole and after each hole we will double our money". Paul agrees, knowing that 10cent is a ridiculous number and he can well afford it, even if he loses all the holes. But Paul does not understand the power of the multiplier effect, that coupled with the fact that Mary is an ace golfer means that Paul is in for a very bad day...

Assuming that Mary wins all the holes...

Hole One,	Mary wins	.10cent
Hole Two,	Mary wins	.20cent
Hole Three,	Mary wins	.40cent
Hole Four,	Mary wins	.80cent
Hole Five,	Mary wins	1.60cent
Hole Six,	Mary wins	3.20cent
Hole Seven,	Mary wins	6.40cent
Hole Eight,	Mary wins	12.80cent
Hole Nine,	Mary wins	25.60cent
Hole Ten,	Mary wins	51.20cent
Hole Eleven,	Mary wins	102.40cent
Hole Twelve,	Mary wins	204.80cent
Hole Thirteen,	Mary wins	409.60cent
Hole Fourteen,	Mary wins	819.20cent
Hole Fifteen,	Mary wins	1,638.40cent
Hole Sixteen,	Mary wins	3,276.80cent
Hole Seventeen,	Mary wins	6,553.60cent
Hole Eighteen,	Mary wins	13,107.20cent

How is going to explain that to his wife? The numbers game is a powerful, potent and magic game to play. If Paul had agreed to start the game of golf in accordance to the same rules and with only .20cent per hole he would owe Mary €26,214.40 and if the game had started with €1 per hole, Paul would now be in the red to the total of €131,072.00.

This just sounds like one of those pyramid schemes...
That is a great analogy to describe the banking industry. It is just a ponzi scheme or a sophisticated 'con job', like the old three card trick that is designed for you to lose, but occasionally they let a winner through just to keep the illusion alive. Take a trip to your nearest seaside resort and play the slots there, you will notice that you put in a lot more than you get out. They are designed, programmed, chipped and set up to create that very reality. As the game is currently played YOU CANNOT WIN.

Is there any way to win?
Yes, but you need more information in order to understand the bigger picture and once you have that I will tell you how to turn the tables on the money changers and reset the system in order for a new consciousness to take centre stage.

The smoke and mirrors of fear: this is the most powerful resource every institution has. The banks threaten you (gently, quietly, legally, lawfully and politely) by giving the impression that they can repossess your home. When necessary they will take a home or two to make sure that everyone watching witnesses their power. Of course understanding your true nature, which includes being free and having knowledge of common law, will give you the power to help educate the legal system and the banking system that your home can't be repossessed.

But they are repossessing homes at the moment?
Only from those who don't know what to do. There are many stories of people who are rebutting the sheriff and the Gardai and keeping their homes. Remember, knowledge is power and all the dice fall in the favour of he who knows how and when to throw them.

How do people find the courage to do something?
If you are waiting for the courage, it will never happen. The courage comes after you do it, not before.

The smoke and mirrors of confusion: the best way to disempowered someone is to deny them knowledge. When access to the facts is limited, people are often left with a whirlwind of possibilities, potential outcomes and unknown factors that may swing things in a direction that they do not know how to navigate. The confusion this creates causes people to question their confidence in taking on a battle in which they may lose everything. It also results in a divide and conquer consciousness that prevents people from thinking in terms of the collective where it is truly a case of 'united we stand, divided we fall'.

The smoke and mirrors of bureaucracy: the layers of paperwork, policies and procedures that the banks have adopted in order to hide their secrets are beyond most people's reach. They send customers through so many hoops in order to deal with problems that by the end of the process they are frustrated and worn out. In most cases, the customer fades away with no resolution achieved. Eventually they may just start again with a different institution that will prove to be equally useless and unhelpful.

The smoke and mirrors of government: the banks are supported by the government who are afraid of the banks because they control the money supply. The banks throw legislation in the face of the customer who complains and threatens them with jail, fines and other forms of punishment if they do not comply with the game plan. Everyone knows that the government works for the banks, as can be seen from the recent bailout charade where the ordinary person was left hung out to dry. Similarly with the legal system, this too is managed by government appointed people called judges who work in government owned buildings they call courts. The idea of a judge making an independent judgement when it comes to the banking crisis is wishful thinking at best. Judges tow the party line or risk being kicked out by the tribe.

The smoke and mirrors of judgments and assumptions: the system has been so finely tuned over the centuries that we often default into a world of assumption in relation to the 'powers and authorities' within our country. We assume that we live in a democracy and that those in the top ranks of the banking world are smarter than we are. We worry that without the bank, government and legal system that society would become a place of unmitigated chaos when this is what we are already experiencing because of debt, tax, punishment, suicide, jail, threats, deceit, lies, psychological and emotional turmoil. It would be fair to say that these systems only give us reasons to be untrusting and paranoid because banks, governments and legal systems in their current condition take everything and give nothing back.

Chapter 10

It Is Personal

Did You Know

- The financial crisis is not about the banks, it is about you and your future.
- We can create a different experience of life if we believe that we can.
- The end of the financial system does not mean the end of life, it means that life can begin without debt.

But don't we need the banks and money?

We have created a way of life that depends on the banks and money as a means of getting by. As we now know, these banks are truly fraudsters and money is based on an illusion. The next question is, why do we need a system that steals from the people?

Even so, I am not suggesting that we switch off the banks and switch on a new system over night. It is unlikely that we are ready physically, emotionally, psychologically or mindfully to manage a sudden change of that nature. We should however identify the steps we need to take in order to move closer to manifesting that reality.

Everything in our world relies on the banks to succeed. Even the most profoundly spiritual person, who has passed beyond the illusion of the world, needs to dance the money dance once in a while in order to provide for their essentials. But that does not mean there is nothing beyond it. There is always an option and we have a choice to create whatever is not there. After all, the system that is currently oppressing the Irish nation was once only a thought in someone's head and actioned into experience. We can do the same with a new system that works for all and helps the greedy to realise that they too can be happy, fulfilled, fed and at peace. It seems that most of them are not happy, considering that the game they are playing offers material riches but the price they pay is at a relationship, heart and peace level.

At this stage, financial dependency is so engrained within our mindset that even those who have been badly treated will defend the system. During a recent meeting, a gentleman displayed such a powerful defence of the banks that I had to ask him to calm down. Only moments earlier he explained how his debts already had him in court, resulted in the repossession of his properties and an injunction being taken against him. The banks had also frozen the money in his account and were soon coming after his home. He spoke of his disgust of what was happening, his fear of ending up with nothing and his anger that after fifty eight years living and thirty nine years of hard work his life was in a mess.

This gentleman is a perfect example of how people can be locked in the dependency. Regardless of how bad things had become, he still defended the banks because he felt that if they were to go bust, any hope of moving forward was impossible.

The idea of changing our lives seems almost impossible...

We must first understand that life is only a reflection of who we are, so that whatever is going on within us, is what we see around us. We need to look beyond what has been set out as a norm and listen to the uplifting inner voices that have been silenced. By doing so, we will soon change ourselves from within and experience this change everywhere. It is an active process and not something that just happens but is created by us.

It appears that we are spending a lot of time and energy looking for reasons to find fault with the systems, when there is no need to do so in order to make a change. We just need to ask whether the system supports our growth, development and freedom from a life of limitation.

What do you want for your life, your children and for their children? There is much more to this world than accumulating riches. There was a time when we all jumped on the express train to wealth and then asked what happened when it disappeared... well, what happened? The future is in our hands and we can create whatever change is necessary in order to tune into an authentic experience of living. Are we going to choose to be beaten down until we have nothing left, other than the frail shadow of a once colourful dream, or are we going to connect with the true needs of our hearts and minds?

Imagine that your life is one of peace where you do not need to own an expensive car or the biggest house on the road. Allow yourself to fantasise of a life complete as you are, filled with self validation and a desire only to help the world around you become the best version of itself that it can be.

At this point, exposing the corruption within the banking system is useless if only driven by a desire to witness its collapse, any desire to expose the banking game needs to come from an intention to find our true purpose, power and place in the universe. Right now, there is a need to show the world what is happening so that we can lift our head out of the sand and own our own responsibility for where we find ourselves. The change that we are looking for is not a child of clever thinking or a branch from the tree of revenge, it is a conscious decision to become an

active part of a solution that needs to have forgiveness, fairness, compassion and acceptance at its core.
It is also important to acknowledge the anger and exhaustion that many people are feeling, but it is also our choice to move beyond it and to reinvent ourselves from the mistakes we have made.

But it is not fair that so many people are in so much trouble and cannot find a way out?
I agree it is not fair! The people of Ireland simply dreamed a dream and trusted those they put in the place of authority to make sure that what was needed to support their dreams was provided; no doubt that was abused, the people were abused and greed took over. There are very few people who didn't experience the almost immediate collapse that happened and as things are today they will be living with the consequences for a very long time. This is why we need to make some big decisions and have some very serious conversations. We need to ask the big questions and go where we have never gone before. We need to accept the past that has left us terrified of the future and realise that life begins here and now. Not at the end of the recession, not at the collapse of the banks and certainly not when we are clear of debt and ready to move on. If we wait for those things to make the change we will never know change, we will only know more of what we are experiencing today. It is in the now that life is happening and once we accept that the change begins... it is as a result of this that we will move beyond the recession, it is as a result of living in

the now that we will realise what we need the most and the banks will no longer be able to do what they have been doing and it is this present moment awareness that will give us a new start with no debt.

What are the big questions we need to ask?

What do I need in my life? Throughout my years working in the field of personal development I have found that the answer to that question is always the same: I need peace, fun, love, joy, time out, my friends and family around me. I need to move beyond negative thinking, to be at rest, to accept myself and stop trying to be someone else just to please others. I need to see the good in as many people as possible and experience the oneness of all things. I need to walk more in the country, to learn to appreciate the small things in life, to sing and dance and know that there is a reason for my being here. I need to be gentle with myself, to believe that I am as important as anyone else, to be inspired and to inspire others. I need to feel alive, to know who I am, to experience the spirit within, to laugh at myself, to heal my pain and to know that I am enough.

Never have I heard anyone say that they need money, a big house, car, or to travel the world in business class, nor did they need to be better than everyone else. This is only what people want because they believe these things will give them peace, fun, love, joy, time out, friends and family around them, positive thinking, rest, self acceptance, the experience of oneness, appreciation of the small things in life, time to sing and dance, a

reason for their being here, the capacity to be gentle with themselves, inspiration, a feeling of being alive, knowledge of the spirit within, laughter and knowing that they are good enough.
Everything that you 'NEED' in life comes from within. In fact, the more you seek them in the external world the greater the emptiness you feel, because as soon as you get them you feel further away from your true self and the fulfilment of your true needs.

After we have answered the question 'what do I need', what then?
Then you ask about what you believe in and why? You also ask what you have learned from these beliefs and what you must let go of. Question everything: banks, money, religion, medicine and the legal and health systems, politics and those in the political game, even the education system that is teaching your children. It is by asking powerful questions you will discover the answers will set you free.

Is there not a risk that we will discover that we've got it all wrong so far?
Perhaps, but would you not like to know that now, so that you can make the changes that give you a sense of what life is really about?

Is this not going a bit too deep? After all I was only asking about how I can find my way out of the mess I am in with the banks.

To understand what I am saying you need to listen with your heart and not just your head. If you switch on the head and switch off the heart then yes, it is a bit too deep and will not truly get what this discussion has to offer. But if you involve the whole self you will certainly get it and, even if nobody else does, it will set you free, before you know it you will be dealing with life in a very different way than before. All of a sudden you will not be worrying about things that before caused you sleepless nights; you will not be suffering from anxiety, depression won't come knocking, arguments won't happen anymore and you will feel younger, fitter and inspired most days.

Of course, you can just stay in the mindset that you are currently in and continue on the path you are currently on. Everything in your life is down to you and your choices.

The fear for some is so great that they would rather continue in their ignorance. We have been programmed to shut down and switch off rather than stand alone and risk being different, we are trained to stay within the tribal thinking or risk being abandoned, and ridiculed. Your future is your choice.

Chapter 11

It Is The Law

Did You Know

- The legal system has nothing to do with right or wrong. It is about the Law and the Law is not about right or wrong.

- Man is not there to serve the Law, the Law is there to serve man, but that is not what the system wants you to think.

- The solicitors, barristers and judges of Ireland are taking you to court and finding against you in favour of the banks that they themselves are in debt to. Is that not a conflict of interest?

Surely the legal system is there to help the people of a country?
Not necessarily.

Why not?
Because the legal system is designed to protect itself and not the people who challenge it! Think about it... it is (the legal system) designed to implement the law and the law that is written in front of him/her is the first port of call when you challenge a judge, solicitor or barrister. No matter what your argument or your personal circumstances, the legal person will respond with what the laws say. If it does not allow for what you are saying, you are asked to take another approach.

But is a solicitor or a barrister not there to defend you?
In theory, they are, but they are also tied up in their membership to the Law Society which governs the system and facilitates the game they are playing. For this reason they will not challenge it, stand up against it or speak about the truth of what is happening and they certainly will not inform the general public of how they can challenge it without legal help.

Can we challenge it without legal help?
Of course you can but you need to know what you are doing or you will be given benefit.

What's benefit?
Jail.

How is Jail a benefit?
It may not seem like a benefit to you but to the legal person sitting behind the big 'alter like' table, jail is a benefit. The judge's way of thinking is simple. If you challenge him because you think you are being treated unfairly, after the third or fourth objection from you, the judge feels that you are not respecting him nor listening to him. He may feel that his authority is being challenged and you believe that you are equal to him. At this point he will say 'Mr. Smith, you are testing my patience, I have told you that your argument is not sufficient and you seem unable to produce anything else to make me think differently'. The fact that you may be right is irrelevant, if you cannot prove it with evidence, you lose. You might tell the judge that he is being unfair and you feel that he is working against you. At this stage he will pull out the old shut up or else routine by letting you know that you can be held in contempt if you insist on speaking out of turn. Here is what he is thinking... 'Mr. Smith, I am the boss and what I say goes in this court. You may think you have a right to challenge me, but your challenging me is a privilege and if you continue I will revoke your privilege and give you some benefit of time in the big hotel; an all expenses paid holiday with a private room, all your meals supplied and no bills. There you can realise that the next time you come before me you will not be foolish enough to think that what you have to say

matters or counts for anything.' What he really says sounds very different but the result is the same.

But he cannot do that, can he?
Who is going to disagree with him unless they too want a free holiday in the all expenses paid hotel?

Maybe they would think differently if they had to sit before the court as a defendant and have the banks chasing them for money?
Maybe. It appears that many of the country's judges are in hock to the banks as a result of property deals that went bad when the downturn hit.

So it is one rule for them and another rule for us?
It would seem so.

What happens if a person defends themselves in a court and tells the judge about the securitization process and the fact that the bank sold the loan, or if I explain the assets/liability reality that shows I owe nothing?
Unfortunately the answer is not as inspiring as it is frustrating. Here are a few real life experiences that are directly connected to your question.
Paul went into court to defend himself against the bank's claim that he owed them money. During the case Paul said that the law states the bank must produce the original mortgage documents with the original wet ink signature (the original signature that was signed in pen is

provided and not a copy of the document which has a copy of the signature on it). The judge agreed and sent the bank off to get the original document with the original signature. Once the case resumed the defendant requested to see the document which he claimed was only signed by the defendant and his wife and not by all parties. It was Paul's understanding that according to Irish Law the bank should also have signed the 'contract', which is really just an agreement. The judge agreed that as a point of law the contract should be signed by all parties.

So he won his case on a technicality then, right?
No, the judge continued 'but you still borrowed the money so you should repay it'. At this stage the defendant was thrown from his focus and began to engage with the judge in a conversation about the money and he lost sight of the original argument about the signature. He answered 'no, I didn't get the money'. The judge was confused and claimed that he must have as he bought the property with the money that the bank provided. The defendant continued to explain to the judge that he had not received money from the bank, further explaining that the bank returned to him the money he had created and that it was he who had funded the capital that had created the loan. The judge's answer was amazing. He said, 'I don't understand all that and it makes no sense to me'. After only a few minutes of making this statement the judge found in favour of the plaintiff and Paul lost his property.

I don't understand, the judge agreed that the contract should be signed by both parties, if not I would expect that the contract was invalid and Paul could not be held liable...

However, Paul was afraid to demand the issue of the unsigned contract be addressed with more than a simple grunt and a swift move into the distraction created by the judge. He argued with the judge that he did not get money from the bank and that the property was bought with 'money' that he himself created and there was no loan given only paperwork to suggest that a loan was given. In response the judge threw the argument aside with his only defence being 'I don't understand that'. Paul should really have stood his ground in that moment and demanded that the case be sent to a higher court or at least to another court where the judge did understand the argument. It makes perfect sense to claim that the judge had no right to find in the banks favour if he could not even understand the argument of the defence. If nothing else, he should have instructed Paul to explain it further so that he could understand it.

This is a perfect example of how indifferent a judge can be to the defendant's cause. In response to Paul's argument he merely defaulted into the how things are done around here response and by making a number of assumptions about the defendant, he skipped down the road of least resistance.

If the defendant was given true equality and the right to defend his position, the court would make it its business to fully understand both sides of the argument before coming to a conclusion. But the judge just said “I don’t understand” and moved on, which in effect was his way of dismissing the argument in order to find in favour of the bank. Do not forget that the bank is now owned by the government and the government pay the judge’s salary.

Is there another example?
Yes. James went into the court and asked the judge to request the plaintiff to produce the original documents with the original wet ink signature. They returned to the court with no original documents but armed only with a letter from the receiver, that is the accountancy firm that were appointed to take over James’ property. The letter was written and signed by the receiver stating that they were not expecting to be asked for the original documents and as they have not had the time to get them from the files - the letter was supporting their assurance that the copy of the ‘contract’ produced in the court was a true copy of the true original. The judge accepted this letter as proof that the contract provided was the real thing. Ten minutes later James lost his home and was given only a number of months to get out.

But you said that the original should be produced in the court.
So it should, but the judge decided to overlook that fact.

Why did the judge not insist on the original document be produced?

The courts are working hard not to let out the truth. Besides, the judge will claim that he is only there to listen to both sides of the argument and then make a judgment based on the facts.

But he didn't listen to Paul when he explained about the money being created and not loaned.
I did not say the judge would listen to all sides of the argument, only that they claim that that is what they do.

Is there another example?
Well there was a curious something that happened at the end of James' case.

What was that?
James had been sending in a number of letters to the bank asking them to produce certain documents in order to support their claim that he owed them money. You see, James had begun to learn about the banking and legal systems and was beginning to ask for specific things from the bank. At the end of the case the judge stated that the court had become aware that many such letters were being sent into the banks and were being produced in the courts and 'people' were to be very clear that these letters held no weight in the court as they were printed out and signed by the sender, but as they were not penned by the same they were of no value.

What was strange about that?

Because the courts claim is that a letter printed out and signed but not written by the signing party hold no weight in the court. When is the last time you received a letter from your bank that was not a standard letter, printed out and not even signed. If the courts argument is worthy of hearing, which it is my opinion it is not, then the banks' letters to you hold no weight and should not be allowed to be used as evidence a court of law.

So then there is no way for a person to win if he goes into court on his own.

At the moment that seems to be the truth but that does not mean it cannot be done. The person going in alone needs to know what they are doing and that takes work, time, effort and resources. Remember this; man is not there to serve the law, the law is there to serve man.

'man is not there to serve the law, the law is there to serve man'

It seems to be opposite.

That is because at the moment man is a servant to the law, solicitors, barristers and judges but soon what is right and fair will come to the surface. There are things about life and the true nature of those who walk the planet that many in the banking and legal systems know nothing about. They have been so focused on their own trip to glory that they have missed the evolution that has been going on around them. The fear that once fuelled their engine is not so present anymore and their assumption that people are stupid is now in question, the world is now educated, courageous and strong. We have past the age of being run from our land on the word of a system that favours the wealthy and the elite.

In a recent 'off the record' conversation with a judge I asked 'do I not have the right as a free person born into a free land to stand up and defend myself if I believe and know that the court is not being fair to me and if I know that the court is wrong?' The judge to my amazement answered 'the first thing you have to realise is that you are not free'. As the conversation went on I continued to ask what were obviously uncomfortable

'They have been so focused on their own trip to glory that they have missed the evolution that has been going on around them'

questions of the judge, a short while later with a smirk on his face he informed me that I was somewhat of an annoyance to him and if I were in his court I would find myself in contempt i.e. I would possibly get benefit (a short stay in his free hotel), and we are supposed to believe that a judge is impartial and does not allow his own agenda onto the playing field. It seems to me that a lot of people are losing their cases as a result of agendas other than what is right or wrong.

You talked a bit about contracts. Can you say something about legal contracts in relation to debt?
In order for an agreement to be fully legal and lawful there must be a contract in place between all parties. In matters such as mortgages, credit cards, loans, car finances and overdraft like there is more than a hand shake required. All parties must enter into a contract and the contract must be written and signed by all parties. That way nothing is refutable and the terms are clearly expressed on paper with the signatures for all to witness, so that if a disagreement happens, both parties can refer to the same in order to resolve the issues.

Does that not fly in the face of all that you are saying?
Not at all, why would it?

Because we all have contracts with the banks for our mortgages and if the contract is the document that states the terms then the banks have us in a corner.

You do not have a contract, you have an agreement. Look at your paperwork from the bank. Nowhere is the word 'contract' written, only 'agreement'.

Is there a difference in a contract and an agreement?
There is a significant difference. To start with the word 'contract' starts with a 'c' and the word agreement starts with an 'a'. If you go through the spelling of each word you will notice that they are different.

That is a ridiculous argument.
On the contrary, it is the first step in a process of critical thinking that will set you free from the legal and financial games of life.

Please continue.
First of all, a contract and an agreement express different things in law where one word can make the difference between winning or losing an argument. Even though the courts will claim that a copy of the original agreement, a copy of the loan offer and of the letter of approval make up your contract, they do not. In fact, I have a recorded telephone conversation with the legal department of one of Ireland's main banks where they confirm that 'there are no contracts in relation to mortgages'. Now can you tell me how you can be in breach of a contract that does not exist? The whole thing is a game that has so much political and legal power behind that it that is seems impossible to penetrate. Interestingly, if you did have a contract it is not legally or lawfully enforceable.

Why not?
The contract must have valuable consideration which means that something of an equal value must be transacted in order for it to be considered fair and equal to all parties.

So what did you bring to the table when you entered the agreement with the bank?
I brought my signature which they lodged and which created the money for the house purchase.

What did the bank bring to the table?
Nothing, although they did try to mislead me by giving the impression that they were providing the money, which I now know they didn't. How could they have provided the money for everyone's loans? They just didn't have it.

That is one reason why the hypothetical contract would be null and void. What about a meeting of minds? This means that you and the bank understood the obligations, duties and rights of each other in relation to the agreement you were entering into.

Did you fully understand your obligations, duties and rights at the time of entering into an agreement with the bank?
How could I? They wrote the rules and regulations and then lied to me about what was happening. How could that be a meeting of the minds?

What about full disclosure?
This means that the bank fully disclosed to you everything in relation to the agreement that you were entering into. They explained what was happening and why. They also discussed how the money was being created and the true process of lodging the promissory note coupled with the fact that the asset book would be opened in direct relationship to a liability book for the alleged loan. It means that they covered all the terms and conditions of the agreement and informed you that you have a legal right to change any that you did not like, which would be part of the process of reaching an agreement that worked for all parties. Full disclosure means that they explain the true intent behind the agreement and the detail that in the future third parties may enter the agreement as a result of your loan being sold off. It also means that you will be notified in writing to give consideration to the position of that third party. Anything there sound familiar?

So these are the conditions that exist in order for a contract to be lawful?
Yes. You can read it in any introduction to law book.

So who is the bank that is taking people to court?
The bank is a legal fiction because it cannot talk, walk, interact, make a claim or defend. So how can it take you to court?

In that case, would I be right in saying that the bank is represented by the managers and directors?
I would say that they are the people who should be up on the stand answering some serious questions, but as the legal system is designed, all they have to do is send in a representative who gets to argue points of law in relation to what is written in the books. It seems that finding a way to introduce new concepts, experiences and information into the court room is a privilege held only for those who are part of the system.

If this is so, what can we do?
Just because it is the way it has always been done, it does not mean it is right.

But if I am the injured party, how do I get a chance to argue my case in a way that will call the banks to justice?
Again, you are assuming that the courts are about justice. The courts are about the law that is written and not about justice. Everything in the legal system is about holding up the legal system and maintaining those in positions of power.

What about taking the bank directors to court? We know that they caused the current economic difficulties including reckless lending, misleading clients, withholding facts, lying, covering up the truth about how their business was done?

There is a great opportunity for people to challenge the directors directly and I am amazed that it has not happened yet. The directors of any organisation have a legal responsibility to ensure that they run the business ethically and with integrity. Here is the response from the Minister for Finance to a question of this nature in December 2011: Parliamentary Question Ref Number: 40666/11

> *"as regards the companies act, financial institutions are in the same position as all other companies"*

There are laws in place to protect people from being mislead, misrepresented and lied to, but it seems that the higher up the ladder you are the greater you are protected. The irony is that the governments funded the banks when the downturn hit and left the average person with less money, more taxes and little chance of legal support. There has been no government minister who has stood up for the people of Ireland and demanded support for them. Instead, they have bowed to the demands of the European Central Bank, while many medicate themselves to cope with the stress or hang themselves to escape the fear.

So if the judges are also in debt to the same banks that are taking people to court why don't the solicitors and barristers highlight this in their defence?

Because they are also in debt to the same institutions and are often in a client/solicitor relationship with the banks themselves. Take Bill, who is a solicitor representing you against Bank of Ireland for which you are paying him five thousand euro but Bank of Ireland is also Bill's client and he will soon represent them against those they have brought to court. This time however Bill is earning five thousand euro or more per week from the Bank. Now who do you think has Bill's loyalty, you or Bank of Ireland? Recently a solicitor relayed to me that the banking and mortgage crisis is a 'cash cow' for all those in the legal profession. How heartening to know that the current economic cloud has a silver lining for someone.

What are the things that you can ask the bank for in order to get some information to defend your case?

The first is a copy of the 'contract' between yourself and the bank. Of course you will not receive it because it does not exist. But ask for it anyway, just to see what they send back.

What will they send?

They will send you a copy of the agreement you signed, but an agreement is not a contract.

Is there anything else?

Request a copy of an invoice for the alleged amount outstanding. In this way you are asking the bank to create a legal document that claims you owe them money. The invoice is a powerful piece of paper because it states that you are in contract with the organisation for the amount on the invoice. It also highlights the good and services provided in the transaction which is signed by the person making the claim. However, prepare to be empty handed. Have you ever received an invoice from the bank for all the business you have done with them over the years?

No.
Isn't it strange that the bank will not issue an invoice for the money you allegedly owe them?

Why not?
They will suggest that invoices are not issued for VAT reasons and because they have never issued invoices in the past but the reality is that when they fill in the description of goods and services provided there is nothing to include. The bank provided nothing to you and they know it. Because of this they cannot request payment with an invoice. That would be extortion i.e. trying to get money from you for no reason, giving the impression that you actually owe something. When the bank knows that you owe them nothing.

How are they getting away with it then?
Because they have the government, the police, judges, the solicitors and jail on their side working in their favour, not to mention your fear, that is keeping you in your place.

Do banks have licences in Ireland?

Banks are required to have a licence to do business in Ireland that is written up and governed by the Central Bank of Ireland which has the Minister of Finance as its only shareholder. So in effect the system writes up and creates the licence. Here is what the Minster for Finance said about bank licences when it was presented to him in Parliamentary Questions ref: 40669/11

"Copies of bank licences are not available to the public"

It appears that the system is so corrupt they will not even allow the public to view the licences used by the same banks that are ripping off the country.

Who is governing them and making sure they do their job right?

The Central Bank say that they are responsible for regulating banking according to the regulation that they themselves create, the same regulations that have a hole in them big enough to sink the Titanic. These people are corporate monsters interested only in making money off the back of the ordinary worker.

How can it be fair to bailout an organisation called a 'bank' that when many other organisations are being ignored? Is a bank a special kind of company that deserves priority treatment?

The bank is no more special than any other organisation or company. The fact is that the government needs them, and albeit that the government now supposedly own the banks the truth is that the banks are bigger, stronger, more powerful and better connected than the government and they continue to march to the beat of their own drum. Having a government that is happy to allow this to continue out of fear of losing power doesn't help either.

Do you think the government is that scared of the banks?
Yes, because otherwise we would not be in the mess we are in now. All it takes is a bit of brass, a free thinking mindset, an innovative approach and enough love for your people to find a way forward. From what we have seen so far, none of the above exist with the current administration, while the previous crowd made a more than significant contribution to the crises. More interested in being 'bankers' than in protecting and supporting their people, their close relationship with the financial sector may have cost us our sovereignty. Potential future governments do not look too inspiring either.

What are the legal consequences for the bank and the client if one or the other breaches the terms of the agreement?
You lose your home and the bank gets a bailout. You are still assuming that there is a system of monitoring in place to ensure that the banks do not breach their conditions of licence. You need to accept that there is no system to monitor this and anyone who tells you there is,

is referring to something that exists in name only. Again, look at the economy, does it look to you that anyone was keeping a watchful eye? Does it appear that a monitoring system in place? If there was, we would not be in this position.

If a bank has been operating in breach of one or more of the conditions of their licence, how can 'agreements' they have entered into while doing so be legally binding?

If everything was being operated in a fair and honest fashion they would not be legally valid but we must remember that the system is wrong, bent, and corrupt. Right now the most important thing we need to do is to accept that the banks have been lying to the people of Ireland and the world. Until that happens we be delayed from moving forward.

Is the legal system corrupt and are solicitors, barristers and judges involved in the business of law to the point that they are preventing people from having a fair chance at creating a better experience of life?

Although few people believe that the entire legal system is corrupt, many have lost faith and are beginning to question the ethics of those who claim to work for the good of the country.

'the government are not going to discuss the undiscussable any time soon'

Chapter 12

In A Nut Shell

Did You Know

- Life is built on perception.
- You create your own reality.
- We have the power to change everything.

There is a lot of information coming my way and I want to make sure I am getting the full picture. Let me recap on what I am learning...

I was under the impression that I had taken a loan from the bank to buy my house but that is not what happened. I simply entered into a relationship in which I created money, and as the intention of the alleged agreement was that the person who funded the capital for the loan is repaid in full, I borrowed nothing. The bank simply repaid me with a financial instrument called a cheque (or an electronic transfer) the full amount of which I created with a promissory note. This happened because the bank must open not only an asset book, which creates the credit from the promissory note, but also a liability book for the same transaction. They now owe the money that was created via the lodgement of the promissory note to the person who created the capital that funded the loan. This is a loan that we now know was just an exchange of borrowings in order for money to be created. To prove this, I get the bank to produce the bookkeeping entries that are related to my mortgage, and in examining these entries I will see how the asset book cancels out the liability book and therefore the debt cannot exist. So I owe nothing.

If the bank claims that they funded the loan I ask what money was used to fund it, given that the banks does not have the capital available to fund all loans. It only exists on a computer screen. Having said that, even if they could prove that they funded the loan I still owe them nothing because the bank bailout replaced their lack of funds which, in turn, resulted in the clearance of all debts. Remember that it is the tax payer's money into the future that repays this bailout fund which means that the entire country is clearing the debt that was used to clear the banks debts. The result of which is a collective loan. Regardless of which, the banks continue to come after us for alleged 'individual' loans.

Coupled with which, the banks have sold off many of our mortgages and other loans in a process known as securitisation. For this reason we are not responsible for them any longer. Of course this is fascinating information, but it is of no practical use because the loans never existed. Why? Because we created the capital that funded the 'loan' in the first place. When the banks handed over the financial instrument known as a cheque or electronic transfer, we were only repaid the money that we created. Interestingly the Minister for Finance responded in the Dail to a number of questions that related to securitisation and he stated: *'the customer will not be aware that their mortgage has been funded in this way'* (Parliamentary Questions 8/02/2012 ref: 6982/12, 6989/12, 6990/12, 6991/12)

At this point we see that the real game was never about the individual 'loans', but the illusion these 'loans' created that allowed the banks to amass fortunes from lending based on the fractional reserve system that states that a bank can loan out up to ten times what their asset book is worth. This means that my €300,000.00 'loan' was worth up to €3,000,000.00 to the bank but only because they

misled me and everyone else into thinking that the loan we took actually existed.
We now know that the banks are acting under a lie when they take people to court and repossess their properties. This lie is that the borrower has breached a contract when there was never a contact to begin with and even if there was, it would be null and void by virtue of the fact that no loan was taken by the 'borrower'. The result is that any repayments made were through extortion. Reason says that not only was there no loan and that I do not owe the banks any money, but the banks now owe me the full amount of what I paid them since the 'alleged loan' was agreed.

However, as this game continues the banks are declaring loans as defaulted and the idea of getting a judgment against the 'borrower' allows the bank to claim a tax write off in relation to the 'losses' they suffered. Furthermore, these banks have their loan books insured and are claiming against default insurance policies that were put in place in order to make sure that the "loan' is paid up in full. We are now aware that not only are these loans being paid in full but they have been paid for many times over once we consider the sales price in the securitisation process, the bailout that was received, the court judgments against the borrower, the continued demand that the borrower pays out on the 'alleged' balance of loan once the banks have sold off the property they have repossessed, the tax right off and the insurance claim that internally settles the 'bad debt'.

However, in spite of the fact that this banking "con job" is hidden in full view, the Irish people have no access to the support and advice that they need because the solicitors and barristers are protecting themselves, the legal system that they have signed up to, as well as their well-heeled clients who want to take from us our commercial properties, homes, businesses, life savings and investments. Then there is the fact that the legal system has at its head government appointed representatives and Judges who are themselves in debt to the same institutions. They too assume that once the law says something, that that something can never be changed. It is into this black hole that everyone in the country falls and there is nothing left to do only watch the global transfer of wealth continue in accordance with the European agenda. Meanwhile the people of Ireland are being abandoned to a situation that cannot be resolved at any level for many generations, if at all.

The idea of the system allowing the people of Ireland to find a way out of this situation seems improbable, as the governmental system also creates the legal reality, the prisons and the revenue offices. It is controlled by the banks themselves that blindly follows the agenda for a united states of Europe. We now know that Ireland's financial sovereignty is being dictated by Europe even though it was Europe that got us into this mess in the first place. Let us remember that Ireland voted 'NO' to the Lisbon Treaty but the government of the time and Europe said 'sorry, wrong answer, vote again' and they enforced a second vote that gave them the result they wanted.

This country now finds itself in serious trouble in relation to the money it owes to Europe, which was lent under the same conditions under which individuals 'borrowed' for their own homes and businesses. Therefore money that Ireland allegedly owes Europe does not exist either, but by making us pay, the government can pay Europe and the few people at the top of the pyramid who end up with everything. The madness continues when we reflect on the massive amount of the money (that doesn't exist in real terms) that is being paid to unsecured bondholders. Another word for the bond holder is 'gambler', and with that in mind the people of Ireland are now broke as we pay off the gambling debts of a few people who knew that they could not lose out, and just in case there are a few brave souls who speak out, the legal system will give them 'benefit' until they see it from the "right" perspective. It is unbelievable but unfortunately it seems to be the truth.

Chapter 13

For Doubting Thomas

The following article shows the level of corruption that lies at the heart of the legal system.

Herald – November 2011 - Cormac Murphy

High Court chief raps solicitors' lies in debt cases

ONE of the country's top ranking legal professionals has described solicitors' sworn statements in relation to debt recovery as "not generally reliable".

Master of the High Court Edmund Honohan said that some lawyers had "debased" the concept of the affidavit.

In a judgment, Mr. Honohan SC said solicitors were the group "most frequently found to have only a nodding acquaintance with the truth" when it came to swearing affidavits.

Mr. Honohan, the brother of Central Bank governor Patrick Honohan, had attacked court procedures relating to debt recovery.

He spoke out against the fairness of allowing banks to get judgment orders against borrowers without a full hearing taking place.

He said he believed the procedures breached the right to fair trial provisions of the European Convention on Human Rights Act 2003.

Many applications are granted on the sworn evidence from creditors' solicitors that a defendant has no defense, Mr. Honohan noted.

Law Society director general Ken Murphy has hit back at the comments saying they amounted to a "vicious side-swipe" against the entire solicitors' profession. He said if Mr. Honohan has evidence of lawyers falsely swearing affidavits he should report it for investigation by the Law Society or refer it directly to the president of the High Court.

Mr. Murphy said the comment, as reported, "is unworthy of anyone involved in the administration of justice.

"The sworn evidence of solicitors is rightly accepted by judges in all courts every day," he added.

Mr. Murphy accused the master of a sweeping smear against the profession.

"It is this allegation that has no acquaintance – nodding or otherwise – with the truth," he wrote in a letter published in the Irish Times today.

"Although the Master of the High Court is not a judge, this reported branding of the solicitors' profession as frequently untruthful in their dealings with the courts is unworthy of anyone involved in the administration of justice," Mr. Murphy insisted.

David Hall of New Beginning, which helps out homeowners in repossession cases before the courts, backed Mr. Honohan's remarks about the imbalance between banks and borrowers.

He told the Herald the same can happen with people's homes "if you don't give a defense and you can't afford legal representation or you're too scared to go to court, "The process goes on without you. You're served with the papers, you're given every opportunity to come, but a bank is a very big organisation that has full administrative and legal staff. You're at a huge disadvantage when it comes to this process in relation to a bank.

Authority

"They have all the power and authority to come into court whereby the average person can't afford that and most certainly a person in financial difficulty is not going to be able to afford legal representation," Mr. Hall added.

At the moment, a defendant has one opportunity to make their case in a crowded court, Mr. Honohan stated.

Debtors representing themselves could be confused and unaware they should have a sworn affidavit, the master said.

If a defendant is refused leave to defend, they have effectively lost the case with only a right of appeal to the Supreme Court, he added.

This article is a perfect example of throwing crumbs to the peasants. If, every so often a little food is thrown in the direction of the hungry and the desperate to keep them thinking there is more on the way. The truth is that the corruption is happening and nothing is happening to stop it. You would think that if the master of the high court highlighted corruption in the legal system that the government would immediately intervene to protect the people? Apparently not.

The following day the master of the court responded to the demand to offer evidence in relation to such a claim as the article highlights. He produced a number of affidavits and named names. Do you think those named have been reprimanded and prevented from practising? Of course not because the system turns a blind eye even after it acknowledges that they lie on sworn affidavits. Incidentally, the Master of the Courts is a brother of the Governor of the Central Bank... how cosy!

In the following article you will read that the legal system knows that the banks are attempting to extort money from the people of Ireland by attempting to collect money on debts that have already been written off. You will also see how the media confirms that 'taboo subjects' exist in relation to the general practises of the banks.

> ***Guardian.co.uk - May 2011 – Lisa O'Carroll***
> *Banks driving people to suicide*
> *One of Ireland's most senior high court officials has spoken out about banks hounding people over debt, some of which has already been written off.*
> *The high price of Ireland's deep recession was centre stage today after the master of the high court gave voice to a taboo subject and said banks were driving some borrowers who couldn't repay their debt to "suicide".*
> *Edmund Honohan said some banks who were "cheerleaders of the Celtic Tiger" were*

"reverting to type" and pursuing people to the "bitter end" even when they had no money.

In an extraordinary intervention, he said the "new debt set" have legal rights but some are made to feel like "outlaws".

His remarks come just a fortnight after figures showed that one of the country's biggest suicide crisis centre's, Pieta House, treated 1,063 last year, almost a third more than it did last year.

Joan Freeman, founder and chief executive of the centre, said the recession was creating a sense of despair in the country – with less money and few jobs having a ripple effect on peoples' lives.

He also criticised banks who thought they had the right to pursue borrowers when they themselves had invested as partners and said that in these cases the bank should bear some of the cost of that risk.

"Why should there be an incentive to cause untold harm socially when there is no money at the end of the road?"

He warned that banks should not expect to have it all their own way when pursuing debtors.

"We know which banks were the cheerleaders for the (Celtic) Tiger," he said. "Yet some banks are reverting to type and come to court assuming that the banker always wins anyway. That's not how the law sees it."

He told the Irish Independent that he decided to speak out as many borrowers who cannot

repay their loans, such as mortgages, credit cards and personal loans are being pursued by banks who had already written the loans off.
These aggressive actions in the repossession and bankruptcy courts were just "meaningless accountancy exercises", he said.
Honohan said he had met several widows of people who had been driven to suicide because of the distress of debt.
He told RTE radio it was important to speak out and he thought some people who were feeling suicidal yesterday might be feeling better today because they were not alone.

In the next article you will be reminded how the legal system has no problem moving the goal posts.

Gardai investigating theft and fraud arrest ex-solicitor Byrne
08/12/2011
Struck-off solicitor Thomas Byrne has been arrested today in connection with allegations of deception and theft.
Fraud squad officers detained the disgraced solicitor who is alleged to owe more than €40m to financial institutions and former clients.
Mr Byrne's practice in Walkinstown was shut down by the Law Society in late 2007.
He was struck off the solicitors' roll the following year by order of the High Court after

at emerged he took out multiple mortgages on the same property from a number of lenders.
A Garda spokesman said members of the Garda Bureau of Fraud Investigation examining allegations of deception and theft from several financial institutions and individuals arrested a man in his 40's in the Dublin area this morning.
He is being detained at Irishtown Garda Station under Section 4 of the Criminal Justice Act 1984 as amended.

Where do the People of Ireland go to find a system that works to protect their rights?

Barrister calls on struggling mortgage holders to "take a stand"
A top barrister has called on struggling mortgage holders to come together in a national movement to smash the "divide and conquer" tactics of Irish financial institutions.
Ross Maguire, a co-founder of New Beginning, proposes a "Movement of Mortgage Holders" to harness the power of hundreds of thousands of those in debt to financial institutions, which he accused of pursuing "every ounce of their pound of flesh".
Mr. Maguire's call to arms against banks coincides with figures released last week, which show that the numbers of homeowners in arrears with mortgage payments continues to rise. Almost 100,000 loans are now either in

arrears or have been restructured, according to figures from the Central Bank. The amount in arrears has exceeded €1bn.

The barrister said a great part of the population is "enslaved by debt".

"Left to its own devices, it will bring ruin to our country, impoverish hundreds of thousands and condemn future generations to forced emigration," he told The Sunday Independent.

"Nothing or no-one has ever commanded such power in this State," he added, "and nothing has ever treated our people and institutions of State with such contempt. Not even the Catholic Church in its heyday had such control."

The Government had shown itself "unwilling or unable to take on the financial institutions. The only real option is for people to come together," he said.

"The very existence of such a national movement would have re-balanced the relationship. The banks could not continue their plan of divide and conquer, dressed up as the 'case by case' approach".

"They would be held to account — not by some regulator or ombudsman or impotent minister, but by the borrowers themselves."

He continued: "We need to raise our heads and look to the next generation; to come together and claim what is ours. We need to find the courage in ourselves to do more than recognise unfairness. We need to take a stand

The only way that we can make a stand is to stop paying anything to the banks and withdraw all our cash. When this happens and people start speaking the language of freedom and sovereignty, solutions will be found within a matter of weeks.

This next article is an example of what happens when you believe that a 'title' attached to someone's name actually means something.

You may not believe what you are about to read and to think that this article was actually given space in one of Ireland's main broadsheets. Here, a leading psychiatrist suggests that we should drug the people of Ireland through the water supply. However, his sentiments are neither shocking nor new. Many have wondered why the People of Ireland have been so inactive in relation to the financial crisis, but few are aware that adding fluoride to the water numbs the mind and effects our energy levels.

The Irish Times - Friday, December 2, 2011
Psychiatrist calls for lithium to be added to water
GORDON DEEGAN

A consultant psychiatrist last night called on Government to add lithium salts to the public water supply in a bid to lower the suicide rate and depression among the general population.

At a mental health forum on "Depression in Rural Ireland" in Ennistymon, Co Clare, Dr. Moosajee Bhamjee said that "there is growing scientific evidence that adding trace amounts of the drug lithium to a water supply can lower rates of suicide and depression".

Lithium is used by doctors as a mood stabiliser in the treatment for depression.

Dr Bhamjee said: "A recent article in the British Journal of Psychiatry found the beneficial uses of lithium when it was added to the water supply in parts of Texas."

He said the Government should consider a pilot project for a town in Ireland where lithium salts could be added to the water in very small doses and examine the results." He said there was already strong precedent for governments intervening in the operation of public water supply for health benefits by adding fluoride.

Dr. Bhamjee said that a community would not get "hooked" on lithium "because the doses would be so small".

He said: "There are 200,000 people suffering from depression in Ireland and the Government must think of new ways of tackling the problem."

Fine Gael TD and chairman of the Irish Association of Suicidology, Dan Neville, told the forum that the average annual suicide rate in Ireland in the 1960s was 64-65.

He said: "Last year, 483 people died by suicide and if you add the 123 undetermined deaths, the suicide number is over 600."

He said: "This compares to 212 who died by road accidents, which is also unacceptable.

"Research shows during international recessions, the suicide rate increases by 25 per cent. Ireland has the fourth highest youth suicide rate in Europe."

Mr Neville added: "Suicide is the most common death for 15 to 24-year-olds and accounts for more than those who die from cancer and road accidents combined."

The Limerick West deputy said that the attitude in the mental health service towards those with mental health problems should be recovery and not containment.

He said: "Early intervention, you have 90 per cent cure and late intervention you have difficulties for life."

Mr Neville said that with the well-publicised suicide of footballer Gary Speed, it raised contagion or copycat suicide concerns

What a complete ass.....

In the following article you will get an insight into the contradictions, hypocrisies and the double standards that exist in the Irish political system. Is it now time for a commitment to eliminate all that does not work, so we can begin to live with the prospect of waking up to the sound of the voices within saying 'today you can rest the battle is over'.

His royal slyness Kenny can't be trusted
By Gene Kerrigan
Sunday Independent December 11, 2011

Does he think we're eejits? Probably he does. Here's Enda Kenny on his triumphant journey to Brussels: "Ireland's economic security has been defended and protected." It seems that our Taoiseach brought "Ireland's case" to the EU leaders' summit and "placed that firmly on the table" and "our European partners" were fierce impressed, so they were.

Does he think we're living in the Fifties, when citizens were dependent on statements from politicians to know what happened at far-off conferences? Last week's events in Brussels were twittered and blogged by journalists as events unfolded. Anyone could follow developments long before the broadcast media caught up. Deeper analysis followed as the summit ended.

We probably knew what was going on before Enda did and the reality is that "Ireland's case" played no part in events. When the big lads have worked out our role in this latest cunning plan, they will tell Enda and Eamon to jump -- and Enda and Eamon will respectfully ask, "how high?"

I trust Enda Kenny as far as I could throw Pat Rabbitte. Last February, looking for votes, Enda went to Roscommon and promised to maintain services in the local hospital. He raged about "bureaucratic people in a room far away from here", who wanted to do the hospital down. So, it was important to elect Enda because, "we are committed to maintaining the services in Roscommon County Hospital".

In July, as he set about removing services from the hospital, he denied to RTE that he'd made such a promise. Next day, RTE broadcast a tape of Enda making his promise to the people of Roscommon.

So repulsed were we by the behaviour of the Fianna Fail shower that the Kenny/Gilmore government was swept into office on a mandate for change. What we got, however, was one discredited brigade of the old politics being was replaced by another.

We are in such deep trouble that the old politics is not working, no matter who is in charge either here or in Europe. With the best will in the world, all these people know how to do is to pull the same switches that got us into this mess. Expecting them to do anything different is like expecting an old Atari console to play Call of Duty MW3. Wrong tool for the job.

During that February election campaign, Kenny went to Millstreet, Co. Cork where he met Joanne O'Riordan, a fifteen year old girl who was born without arms and legs. She is also smart and articulate and wanted an answer. The Fianna Fail shower were taking money from the blind. Ms O'Riordan wanted to know if Kenny would protect the resources assigned to the disabled. He told her that he would. His budget proposals ensured it. "We want that protected."

Last week, Joanne told how she watched the announcement of the latest assault on the disabled, and she and her brother Steve responded with, "Are you actually joking?"
Any of us be blinded or wheelchair bound or have a child born disabled. It is a random thing. Most of us assume we had reached a point in human development where resources that can mitigate disabilities will be available not as a favour but as a right and that in tough times they will be rigorously protected just like Enda Kenny promised Joanne O'Riordan, just ten months prior.
When the cabinet was agreeing to a 53% cut in payments to the young disabled, did Enda forget his promise? Perhaps he forgot there was a camera over his left shoulder as he spoke to Joanne?
The public reacted with revulsion, backbench TDs ran scared and comrade Joan Burton was fingered as the fall guy. She quickly apologised and reversed the disability cuts.
The slyness seeps from everything these people do. A deep, contemptuous cut in benefits due to the disabled was christened a "Labour Activation Measure". Apparently, it would propel those lazy buggers to jump out of their wheelchairs (another "lifestyle choice"?) and take one of the many jobs that are available.
At the same time, government ministers were indefatigable in their defence of the "special advisers" hired at extraordinary rates to --

well, do whatever it is they do. Ciaran Conlon, an old mate of Enda's, was offered €80,000 to advise Richard Bruton. But that was not enough, so they pushed his wage up to €92,000, the highest figure government rules allow. Ciaran emailed his ire at the "ridiculous" delay in paying him what he is worth. Soon after, Enda stepped in to order the pay rules be set aside and Ciaran's salary was increased to €127,000.

It was explained that the government has to pay big salaries in order to attract astonishingly talented people from the private sector. After the banking debacle, I thought we had learned that levels of pay are no signifier of ability. Not that it matters. Eleven of the highest paid "special advisers" are former party hacks, and if any of them had blazed a trail of success through the entrepreneurial forest I must have missed it.

Cuts for the disabled and big bucks for the advisers is not just unfair, it is an essential part of the old politics. On Vincent Browne's programme on TV3 (month and year???), FG TD Kieran O'Donnell was pushed to say how he would be damaged by the budget. At first, it seemed like it had not crossed his mind that he would be affected. Then, he had the honesty to say, "very, very little".

It is accepted that even as ministers wield axes, society's layers of fat must remain virtually untouched. Hack a massive chunk from the vulnerable but shave only a little from the comfortable classes. There is clearly an effort to preserve the establishment untouched that is behind the failure of one cunning but inadequate plan after another.

Thirty years of a failed business model -- call it neoliberal greed or whatever you like, has left a massive knot of unpayable banking debt that has destabilised economies across the continent. The old politics encourage the transfer of the debt to the State resulting in an enforced austerity. Then the books will balance, but this crisis is too big for that and until those who gambled and lost are forced to take their losses there will be no progress.

Last week in Brussels, the politicians did little about the debt, but they did propose new rules to prevent it happening again. It was like officers on the Titanic having a meeting and deciding to create strict new rules on keeping lookout for icebergs whilst ignoring the sinking ship. (Dave Cameron jumped overboard in order to protect London bankers from regulation. "I say, chaps, let's be fair to icebergs, what?")

Enda Kenny was there as part of the furniture. He brought "Ireland's case" and "placed that firmly on the table", where, I am reliably informed, it was discovered the next morning by a cleaner, who emptied it into a waste bin and intends using it for her Christmas shopping.

The following article will further highlight the madness of the games that have been and will continue to be played if we, THE PEOPLE do not do all that is necessary to change life in Ireland, NOW.

> ***David Drumm finally breaks his silence on Anglo, NAMA and the Irish financial crisis – "if my case is indicative of how they are being measured, taxpayers' money is being absolutely destroyed there, day by day by day"***
>
> ***November 27, 2011***
>
> *It is surprising that although David Drumm has been a household name since late 2008 when he resigned as CEO of Anglo Irish Bank (now part of the Irish Bank Resolution Corporation) and although there has been an avalanche of press coverage and at least two books ('The Fitzpatrick Tapes' and 'Anglo Republic'), to date there has been little comment from the man himself. When RTE correspondent, Charlie Bird called on David's family home in Massachusetts last year, all he got was a "have some respect Charlie". There have been volumes of court documents since David filed for bankruptcy in the US in October 2010 as well as some brief phone exchanges, but today in Irishcentral.com, journalist and activist, Niall O'Dowd has what appears to be the most extensive interview yet with the former Anglo CEO who left Ireland in 2009 and has more recently been involved in a*

bitter battle with Anglo about the repayment of loans. The Gardai in Ireland want to speak with him, but apparently do not have a good-enough case to seek his extradition. The Chartered Accountants Regulatory Body has temporarily postponed disciplinary proceedings against David, who is a chartered accountant until the current brouhaha with Anglo has abated. The Office of the Director of Corporate Enforcement is believed to have been building a case against senior former Anglo executives including David and Anglo recently accused David of changing the terms of loan agreements in the case of the Maple Ten. Even the US bankruptcy official handling David's bankruptcy has taken an aggressive view on David's dealings. It is fair to say the 45-year old Dubliner is feeling embattled, and in this extensive interview today, we do get some revelations

(a) NAMA. David says that NAMA was a mistake in "recognizing losses that no other country did, here in the U.S they have just more experience and they had seen this before, no bank was forced to mark all its assets down at a time when you couldn't sell anything. The UK didn't do it, nobody in Europe did it, so Ireland stood alone and by marking this thing down Ireland separated itself down." Elsewhere he says that Pricewaterhouse Coopers (PWC) reviewed the Anglo loan book at the end of 2008, and that Donal O'Connor, who replaced Sean

Fitzpatrick, and Anglo director Lars Bradshaw both reviewed PWC's work, and Anglo concluded that it was correctly showing loan and loss provision values.

(b) Banking supervision in Ireland is portrayed as a bit of a joke and when Anglo got into difficulty in 2008, the Central Bank of Ireland was unable to provide a lender of last resort function. Anglo's balance sheet had gotten too big at €73bn, not unlike its Irish competitors, and even though the loan book was seen as good collateral the central bank was unable to provide short term funding on what were seen to be good assets when the inter-bank funding market froze after the collapse of Lehmans in the middle of September 2008. "they were clueless" says David now. The Regulator and central bank were allegedly telling David that the Department of Finance (where Kevin Cardiff was then responsible for banking in his role as assistant Secretary General) was being relied on for guidance. Anglo did not ask for the guarantee on 30th September 2008 according to David, Anglo just wanted a secured loan from the central bank for €2bn. The first David heard of the guarantee was when he woke up on 30th September. David is seemingly bitter that it was Bank of Ireland and AIB that demanded the blanket guarantee but it was "put at Anglo's door"

(c) Maple Ten. David says that "The financial regulator and the Central Bank were in every meeting with me and other directors of the

bank throughout 2008 and I have to tell you, that was team work, because it [Sean Quinn's 25% shareholding which Sean needed to sell] was a common problem" and "the government, and through its offices through the Central Bank and through the regulator were pushing the bank like hell to fix the problem [Sean Quinn's 25% shareholding which Sean needed to sell]" David says that based on his conversations with John Hurley, the then-governor of the Central Bank of Ireland, the Minister for Finance (Brian Cowen until May 2008 and the late Brian Lenihan thereafter) and "most likely" the Taoiseach (Bertie Ahern until May 2008 and Brian Cowen thereafter) knew about the problem, and by implication the solution of using the Maple Ten, 10 large customers of Anglo, to buy Sean Quinn's shareholding with non-recourse loans. The interview makes a reference to "John Carney" as the governor of the Central Bank of Ireland that looks like a mistake and should refer to "John Hurley". There is also a reference to a "Conn Horgan" but it is not clear who this is. David says the transaction "made sense to Morgan Stanley who were advising us" and that it "made sense to our [Anglo's] legal advisers" What is new is the claim by David that 25% of the loans advanced to the Maple Ten was recourse.

(d) Sean Quinn. David says that, in relation to building up a 25-28% stake in Anglo through

the use of Contracts for Difference (CFDS) "he [Sean Quinn] didn't get advice and he will tell you that himself" Now although David is talking about the use of CFDs, Sean Quinn has a different take on his disastrous stakeholding in Anglo – in his recent statement announcing his bankruptcy in Belfast, Sean Quinn said "recent history has shown that I, like thousands of others in Ireland, incorrectly relied upon the persons who guided Anglo and who wrongfully sought to portray a 'blue chip' Irish Banking stock" But as far as David is concerned "we got this additional spot light on us because of the Quinn perceived vulnerability and the hedge funds in London rightly took a view that if you push, push, push this guy maybe his stock will be sold, the bank will collapse and they get like a payday. He fashioned a rod for his own back and ergo our back, the bank's back"

(e) Sean Fitzpatrick's loans. This looks like dynamite and I reproduce the relevant passage from the interview "Sean Fitzpatrick's loans were not hidden in any way within the bank and they were on the central bank returns. When the financial regulator went into Irish Nationwide it would have been late 2007. They found Sean's loans sitting there. When they came back to the bank in December '07, spoke to Willy McAteer about the loans, he spoke to the chairman and said that he had had discreet finance with Irish Nationwide. The first question they asked Willy was 'is that

reciprocal? Is Sean Fitzpatrick doing it for Michael Fingleton?' The answer was no. The second question 'were there any Companies Act implications or legal issues'? So Willy went to out external council and got a legal opinion that it was not... And then their last question was, 'what are you going to do about it?' and Willy went to Sean and Sean said that he was actually refinancing with the Bank of Ireland, which he was. He was in the process of taking all the loans and getting them away to BOI and they said fine and dropped it."

(f) David Drumm's loans from Anglo. David says he borrowed the money from Anglo to buy shares in Anglo at the request of Anglo, so as to demonstrate confidence in the bank. He blames the current Anglo or IBRC CEO Mike Aynsley for pursuing him relentlessly for the repayment of the loans for which he feels bitter, "it was outrageous to call it in because first of all a bank operating properly would never do that and B they had a contract with me, not to do that in the long term plan." David claims that the assets he was prepared to hand over to Anglo in settlement of the €8-9m of loans were worth USD 10m (€7.6m) but David claims "they couldn't possible settle, it took me a while to accept that" implying there was a get-David-at-all-costs, politically supported approach by Anglo. In respect of the enormous costs being racked up by Anglo in pursuit of David which David claims are in the millions he says "if my case is indicative of

how they [Anglo's management] are being measured, taxpayers' money is being absolutely destroyed there, day by day by day"

(g) David Drumm's future. According to David he has an employment visa which entitles him to US residency, not an investment visa "contrary to what they report in the media, so the visa is not the issue". He wants to stay in the US where he sees opportunities. He complains about media intrusion and literally parking outside his home for days on end. He claims he has moved his two girls to different schools to escape media attention. There is no mention of the serious allegations of fraud made by Anglo or the CARB disciplinary proceedings or the ODCE investigation, but he does make what seems like a sensible point that you would not want to expose yourself and your family to what would almost definitely await David if he returned to Ireland, unless you had no other choice.

***UPDATE: 28th November, 2011. Laura Noonan** at the Irish Independent reports that there has been a response from unidentified "sources close to the bank [Anglo]" to the 10,000-word David Drumm interview. These unidentified sources dismiss David's claims that reckless lending was not the cause of Anglo's collapse as "ridiculous". Presumably these unidentified sources are not working for PwC which certified the loan valuations at the end of 2008, or Donal O'Connor and Lars*

> *Bradshaw which checked PwC's work, or auditors Ernst and Young who signed off the 2008 accounts after presumably sample checking loans and loan documentation. There has been no response from Government, which according to the Drumm interview seems to have been at the heart of the Maple 10 transaction. Maybe we might get an attributed comment later in the day. The Independent does say that it "understands that Anglo would have recouped more from that settlement than the net proceeds the bank expects to get from drawn out bankruptcy proceedings in the United States." Why would a company which we as a nation own 100% take such an uneconomic decision?*

The articles you have just read are a sample of what is available when you begin to investigate the truth behind the government, banks and legal system. Surely to the reasonable mind they support the need for radical change? At this stage it is not enough to trust that we are being taken care of because we are most definitely not and if things are allowed to continue as they are going it will not be long before we are living in a world that is without freedom, joy, peace and prospect of ever experiencing our true nature and purpose. In fact, we could argue that there is little freedom, joy and peace as it is, and the chance of finding a different experience of life are dwindling with each day that passes, with each deal that is agreed with the European bankers and with each new tax that the government slaps on the people. What is left of our world and our life that allows us to know who we truly are? The time has come for us all to become the change we want to see. It is time for action.

Chapter 14

Enda Says...

What does the government say in relation to the current crisis and how it all came about?

The last government of Ireland said that the banks were responsible for the economic collapse and in his address to the people of Ireland in December 2011 An Taoiseach Enda Kenny said to the people of Ireland

"You are not responsible for the crisis"

In January 2012 he said

"The people were seduced by the banks"

So if we are not responsible why are we paying? Why are we losing our homes, our businesses and our life savings?

Is it not strange that the government can answer the demands of Europe but it cannot address the concerns of its own people?

Chapter 15

What Can 'We The People' Do?

Did You Know

- You are more powerful than you have ever imagined.
- The purpose of your life is to be free, to live, to evolve and to discover the greatest version of yourself. It is not the purpose of life to be in debt
- There is nothing you cannot do.

What can we the people do to change things so we can get some normality back to life?

'We The People'

The first thing to take note of is the fact that 'we the people' is a powerful term. 'We' are the people of Ireland and there is little that we cannot do if we realise that together 'we' are a force that is greater than any government, financial system and European idea of an untied state of Europe. One thing is for sure, nothing is going to happen unless we take action with a powerful intent, a serious commitment and an unwavering sense of being in power. The government of Ireland is only in office because they were voted in and as we voted them in we can vote them back out again. Remember, the current government was not voted in because they could do a better job but because of a flaw in the system. When we went to the polls we voted to keep certain people out of office not to vote certain people in, but there was no alternative available other than our current administration. Clearly, if there was, they would be governing now and those who are in office would be sitting on the back benches shouting in opposition. It certainly seems that the purpose of the government has more to do with putting in place what they believe is best, even if their games are not in the best interest of the country. It would be true to say that Enda, Eamon and their band of not so merry men and women have remained true to the manipulation that started this whole mess, although arguably they have gone one better by entering into further discussion with the powers of the world in such a way that 'we the people' are left with no choice, power, freedom or future of our own. Different fingers pressing the same buttons...

"we the people' are left with no choice, no power, no freedom and no future of our own'

- We are allowed to make choices but only if they are within the scope of the rules laid out by the current systems, such as the plan to eliminate any sovereignty that Ireland may have left. Are you aware that you are practically no longer Irish but a European from the country of Ireland?
- You have power but only within the boundaries of that which has been built by the treaties and the shadow constitution.
- The only freedom you have is the freedom to roam around the

playground built within the European courtyard, and such is the size of this courtyard that a short walk in any direction will bring you to the fences that imprison you behind the rules, regulations and legal threats of an evolving one world order. Right now, you have little enough freedom and soon that will soon disappear unless you do what is necessary to change everything that is not working in favour of your evolution and true purpose. The 'little freedom' referred to is the freedom you know yourself. You have as a spirit within a living and breathing flesh and blood body. Do not be foolish enough to think that you are free. You will never be free until you rise up and kick out the prison wardens, take down the walls and rebuild life with a primary focus on what matters most, a quality of life that allows you to feel joy.

- The future you have is one of hard work and a list of eternal bills that are not yours to pay. Your future is really someone else's future. You will simply be the person digging the holes that hold up the same fence that imprisons you. The future is bleak and dark unless you take your place in the army of rising consciousness that is needed to make the experience of life tomorrow different to that of today.

So the first things we need to do is let the current government know that we are finished playing their game.

You also used the word 'normal' in your last question, normal according to what? Who says what the norm is and what the norm is not in the context of 'life', another enormous word that you used in your question.

I am referring to my hope that life can be changed in such a way that we are not always stuck in financial uncertainty in a world that seems to be filled with banks, revenue, the government and the legal system chasing people for what they do not have.

If you want normality then allow what is happening to continue. However if you want a good quality of life where you no longer have to work hard all the time and have nothing at the end of it for yourself then you are seeking a different experience, one that brings freedom, power, belonging, rest, hope, purpose and reason. It is this experience that we are

---

'Perhaps you, I and everyone else in Ireland have been oppressed depressed, anesthetised and silenced for so long that we have actually forgotten the true meaning of life and we have made struggle, pain, fear, powerlessness and debt the norm'?

---

challenged to create. It is time to shine a light on the shadows of normality and let the extraordinary have a chance at guiding us through.

Take a moment to realise that the madness of the legal system, governmental system, banking system, education system, religious and health systems have been the cause of all the troubles we have ever had in this country, and every other country in the world. Imagine what life would be like if we took from each system all the madness and kept only what set people free and brought joy to their lives. Perhaps you, I and everyone else in Ireland have been so oppressed depressed and anesthetised that we have forgotten the true meaning of life and have made struggle, pain, fear, powerlessness and debt the norm?

What are the practical things that we can do to create the change?

A revolution of consciousness is what is needed. Although we have gone beyond the need for violence and anger, we do need action and steadfastness. After all, this is your life we are talking about and the life of your children and grandchildren. Consider your ancestors for a moment who overcame great challenges in order to leave behind a better world. They worked hard so that you could be free and have a better experience of life than they had. Without their willingness to stand tall in the face of adversity we would not have this great nation nor would we have the idea of freedom. Remember that your need for freedom and joy is much more than a human want. It is a spiritual need that is inseparable from who you are, in the same way that the sun's rays are inseparable from the sun and the singer is inseparable from the song.

You are the ancestors of the future. Is it your wish to contribute to the creation of a lineage that is weak and identity less? On reflection, perhaps there is a part of you that will allow the rest of you to realise that the current situation is truly ridiculous, unnecessary and an insult to the gift of life that each of us are responsible for learning to understand and guiding to a place of peace and joy. Is it too much to expect that we might wake up and declare our true nature and purpose to ourselves and the rest of the world? Let us us be the saints and scholars that the future generations speak of.

There are two areas of life that demand action in order to make the change happen:

1. Personal commitments
2. The commitment we make to support each other

Our Own Personal Commitments:

If each of us can agree to the following we may have a chance at making a great leap from oppression and suffering to freedom and in joy.

1. **Stop Being Afraid** and realise that all the things we are running from cannot harm us if we stop running, turn around and face the 'monster'. It does not matter if that monster is a bank, a legal threat, a fear

of poverty, a sense of failure, an anxiety, stress, a sense of being lost or a feeling of powerlessness. The only way to truly kill it is to face it and go to battle with the shadow it casts. We must stop being afraid.

2. **Stop Making Assumptions** and realise that there is a power in questioning everything. It is a fool who takes another man's word that the world is as he says it is. You have as much power, wisdom and strength as anyone that has ever walked this land. Do not assume that things are as you have been told. It is more likely that they are not and all you need to do in order to begin the process of putting an end to your assumptions is look at some of the great 'truths' of life and how they became not so true once the critical eye was cast upon them.
3. **Educate yourself** in knowing who you are and what your true purpose in this world is. Ask powerful questions and seek powerful answers in order to put a true context on your life. Do not accept another's idea of who you are without first seeking the wisdom needed to make your own decisions. Learn to take time out of life in order to find the voice within that will teach you what an illusion versus what 'real' is. Learn to be strong and allow yourself to risk even your own life in the name of truth and in honour of dying after having lived a fulfilled life. Do not allow yourself to be guided through your day according to the rules of someone else's perception, but create your own understanding and seek counsel from your own spirit, the spirit that lives within you is the breath

of life. Do not be fooled into forgetting what matters most and do not be shamed into submission when it is your true destiny to rise higher than the highest point of the heavens and to know joy from a limitless and condition-less experience.

4. **Take Action** and sit no longer in fear. Stand up for what you know to be right and speak your truth. It is better to die from this land in truth and with a meaning than to wait for death to find you in the grip of powerlessness. Make your life count. Give yourself a reason to smile and even if the world thinks you have gone mad celebrate that madness by acknowledging your own sense of purpose.
5. **Dream** your future into existence. Do not wait in one place hoping that a voice from the beyond will tell you what life is, who you are and what your next move is. Create your own reality by connecting with everything that moves in the direction of freedom. Disconnect from anything that makes you feel fear, sad, lonely, hopeless or depressed. Begin now to let go of your past pains, regrets and hurts. Your future depends on you to create it. Make a decision as to what life is to be and make it so. Find those in the world who will support you and walk this path with the full assurance that you and your life have a meaning beyond debt, systems and slavery.
6. **Commit** yourself to all the gifts that life has to offer you so you allow the very force of life to become your greatest teacher. Look to the seasons for inspiration and all of yourself to see that soon after the winter

comes the spring and shortly after that the summer arrives. Right now, you are feeling the darkness of a winter in your life but only through your commitment can you move from this cold and fearful place into a new light, a new beginning and a new life. Be like the daffodils and push your way through the heavy cover of clay and soil that hold you down. Lift your head above the ground of life and scream to the world that you have arrived. Announce to the world that the winter, the frustration, the oppression, the pain and the suffering have passed and make it your business to blossom beyond even your own idea of power and beauty.

7. **Come together as community** and support each other as you agree to step out of the game of life that has been forced upon you. Make it your business to help each other in moments of doubt and fear. Seek friendship and offer love to and receive love from those whose drum beats to rhythm of your heart. Know that you are a spiritual being having a human experience and place the needs of your inner world before the needs of others in the outer world. The outer world is a dream and the world within is reality. Turn within and you will find the strength, wisdom and courage to make great change occur. Think outside the box, step outside the box, close the box and throw it away.

The Commitment We Make to Support Each Other

Take the following steps and you will soon be free of debt in the financial sense but also in every other sense of the word. Make freedom, peace and joy your only focus:

1. **Stop Paying the Banks**. Realise that the game of money is a con and absolutely stop paying the banks anything for mortgages, loans, overdrafts, car finance, credit cards, charges, fines, interest and anything else they claim you owe them – you do not owe them anything. It is time to waken up and look beyond what you have been told. There is a different perception from which you can live. Make the decision today to stop paying. Do not get caught up in worrying how things will work out and how you will manage because everything will work out. It is the nature of life to find a way through everything so once you stop paying, a new way of life and living will emerge. Trust in the process. Your body is made up of billions of cells and all these cells communicate every day to allow you move around, think, act, make decisions and digest your food. So it is with life. Life is made up of waves of potentiality and these waves will create with us a new understanding, experience and level of evolution. The only way to change the system is to stop playing the old game and feeding the old way of doing things. Either you stop paying now or you agree to sign the rest of your life away to debt, cancer, stress, suicide, hard work, depression and a life of no true identity, purpose or meaning.

2. **Build Community.** Find all the people around you who are on this path and connect with them. Support each other and spend time observing the change you are creating once you stop paying the system what it says you owe it... remember, you owe nothing. Put notices up all around your local community letting people know where they can go to get support and to join with you. Don't worry about not having enough knowledge, just take action and stay committed to the action, everything else will organise itself. You simply need to give the natural order of things a chance to express itself and YOU WILL BE TAKEN CARE OF. The reason we are in the mess we are in is because we stopped allowing the natural order to have its say. Humanity has tried to be smarter than nature for too long.... let nature back in the driving seat. Do not be afraid to be the one who steps out. Although you may feel alone you will soon realise that you are not. You are only alone when you play the systems game. Step out and connect with your community. Watch and play as life takes over once again.

3. **Let the government and Europe know you are finished playing their game.** As a community in action send a message to the government and to Europe letting them know that you have stopped playing their game. The system will soon realise that you have taken back your power and it will bend to your demands. Demand and do so without

compromise. Do whatever is necessary for you to let the system know that you are free; send them uncompromising messages from a place of community and connection. Let them know you are not alone. It is not enough to simply say that you are free. Freedom is not something that you do, FREEDOM IS SOMETHING THAT YOU ARE. Become free in your actions, words, and in your deeds and when you speak of your freedom do so with every ounce of passion that lives within you.

4. **Remove the Government and place a group of independent guardians into office** who will do what is needed to guide Ireland back to sovereignity. Begin to realise that life without politics is possible and become a part of the voice that drives the current government out of office, no compromise and no excuses. Create a void, an empty space that we the people fill with those who wish to build a new way of governance and a new way of life. Once the space has been created by clearing out the old, those who are able to bring to Ireland what she needs will show up, you don't know it but they are sitting and waiting this very day for you to take action. Trust in life, in yourself remove the government. Let the country know that a new life is being born into this land. We have been oppressed, occupied, controlled and prevented from having peace and joy for too long.

5. **Create a system of Direct Democracy**. In a free world and as a part of a free system we would have a say in all the decisions that affect and influence our nation, the people of our country and the country itself. Be a part of the commitment to change how we do politics and allow a new system find its way into our lives, one that works for the people, with the people, because of the people and is managed and exercised by the people.

6. **Leave the Euro Zone and begin to print our own money once again.** Print this money as debt free money so debt becomes a thing of the past. Remember the only purpose in interest on money is to create wealth for a small number of people. If we allow ourselves to build a nation that provides for the needs of the people we will not need wealth, for we will be living in the true and ultimate meaning of wealth i.e. having all we need in order to have all we need. What does everyone want in life? Freedom, peace, good health, joy, an experience of life that gives a quality of life and the resources to know that we will not be hungry, that we can live in comfort, give our families what they need and so that we can teach our children how to live a life of happiness. Let us just BE this and create whatever is necessary in order to allow that to BE our experience. It is possible and the only other alternative is what we have now... how is that working for you?

7. **Celebrate Life**. Begin to live with life as a celebration at the heart of everything we do as a community. There has been enough killing, poverty, oppression, toxic secrets, lies, keeping up with the Jones's, anger, shame, guilt, humiliation, loss, pain, suffering, fear and hoping. There has not been enough celebration, belief or passion so let us start again and this time do life without the bullshit and unnecessary distractions from what matters most.

Start now. Pay the banks nothing and connect with everyone in your community who is looking for the support to do the same. It is up to you to take the steps and make the moves.... the rest will follow. Organise all the community gatherings needed so people know they are not alone. Go to the Hill of Tara in Co. Meath and spend some time walking around. There you will be able to connect with the ancestry of your land and you will meet many people who are wakening up to what matters most. Bring your community groups with you; make your action an education. Watch as Ireland rises from the oppression, rise with her, you are one.

Chapter 16

You Are Sovereign

Did You Know

- You are free
- You are free
- You are free

A truly sovereign person lives a life of peace and wishes to do no harm to another.

It seems that the systems and the institutions of life have the whole game sown up and there is little we can do to change that.
You would be very wrong in believing that. There is a lot that we can do and the best place to start is by gaining an understanding of who we are and what exactly is happening in the world around us. We need to know that we are sovereign and understand what that means.

What do you mean I am sovereign, I know that the country has sovereign debt is that the same thing?
This debt is created in the country by the country. In order to understand that you are sovereign you can forget about debt for a while and all the banking stuff as well as the legal stuff. To a sovereign person life is very different because they live with a different set of rules than the rest of society dictates. They recognise the true nature of who they are in the world and everyone as their brother or sister as well as understanding their connection to all things. In your awareness of being sovereign and in your experience of living the sovereign reality, you would have a high level of respect for everyone and everything around you as well as with a sense of responsibility. Although you see things that are flawed in the world you choose to highlight the wrong doing and set it right in the most peaceful way possible. By claiming your sovereignty you are claiming to have

supreme independence and authority over yourself and your life. You are not controlled or managed by anything or anyone else.

How do I become sovereign?
You do not become sovereign, YOU ARE SOVEREIGN. However the way of life you are currently experiencing may not be very supportive of you knowing this and therefore the systems of the institutions will do all they can to keep this truth from you.

I don't understand?
Okay, let's start with a question; who are you? I am Gerard. No that is your name. Who are you? I am a carpenter? No that is what you do. Who are you?
I'm lost already.
Okay, answer this question; from the moment you were born until your parents gave you your name who were you?

I was just a living flesh and blood person.
Great, but you were not Gerard, right?

I guess not.
So what would have happened if your parents never gave you a name?

I don't know, I guess for a start the banks couldn't write to me...

True, but neither could you have taken out a loan with them.

Hmmm, I would be better off if that were the case.
Actually, you are so close to realising the whole purpose of this conversation. You are right, you would have been better off especially when you begin to realise the events behind your name and what it represents.

What do you mean?
Let me tell you a little story. When a ship arrives to the harbour to dock it does so in order to deliver its cargo. Once the ship has birthed and delivered the goods the harbour master will come out and sign the necessary paperwork, a bill of exchange for example. This paperwork gives legal possession of the title of goods to the harbour master and the ship's captain is no longer responsible for it. It is now the property of the new owner who is responsible for making sure that the cargo is used to its full potential and set to work in accordance with the plans that await it. Do you notice anything about the language being used here?

Not really!
The law of the land was developed and designed from the concepts of maritime law, the law of the sea. What you are beginning to hear here is the story of how the government, the legal system and the banks managed to have such an amount of control over you.

Now let us revisit the story but this time we will change some of the details. After going into labour while pregnant your mother went to the hospital and the Doctor ensured that she gave birth and delivered the baby without any injury or harm to either mother or child and if there were complications the Doctor was there to help where possible. Do you see a similarity in language in both stories?

Yes, they are both very similar, there is a doc, a cargo, a birth, a delivery and a place to birth; in one story it is a harbour and in the other it is a hospital.
After you were born the hospital administration person (the harbour master) comes along with the documents to fill in and the registration form to be complete to ensure that the cargo is accounted for. Once those papers were signed and passed back to the administrator you essentially became the property of the state. Your birth certificate stands as the bill of exchange that legally and lawfully handed you over to the ownership of the state. That was the day that you freedom was taken from you. Your parents without even knowing it gave you to the state and agreed that the state had ownership over you.

Why would the state want ownership over me?
Once you become the property of the state the government have the right to take tax from you, to tax your home, your car, your water, your food. They have the right to lock you up in their jails and punish you under their laws. All you need to do is take a step back and see

what has happened. Without registering you under the ownership of the state the government have no rights over you. When you are free you are not subject to the states institutional thinking and you cannot be forced to play by their rules.

But is child registration not about keeping numbers for the census?

Of course not, to keep a track of numbers in the country you simply need to keep a count on the amount of children born into the country each year and subtract that number from the number of deaths in the country in the same year. The census is about controlling information. Read the census form with this in mind and you will see it in a way you have never seen it before. The census is about taking and keeping control of your information in order to manage your life in such a way that the government have control over you. It all boils down to taxes and taking from you as much as is possible.

So it is all about tax and making money?

Isn't everything about making money when it comes to the revenue and the government? They hide their actions behind illusions of social wellbeing and reaching out to the people, but if that was the truth they would easily recognise that the systems are not working and in their true desire to offer a quality of life to the people of the country they would change whatever needed changing in order to ensure that this 'quality' of life was provided.

Once your birth is registered you become a legal fiction under the title of your name. Have you ever noticed that a letter from your solicitor, the bank, the government, the revenue, your credit card company and all other official institutions comes with your name in BLOCK CAPITALS?

Yes actually, I have noticed that. Is that significant?
It is very significant. It is not possible for a company to do business with a living flesh and blood person (that is the person who is unregistered), an unregistered person has no 'identity' in the context of what is needed to do business with them. Only organisations can do business with organisations and once your birth cert is registered you effectively become an organisation. By law you must be written to in capital letters as the institution is not writing to you, they are writing to the legal fiction, the company that you are, the business that you have been registered as. Your PPS number is simply your company number and this follows you throughout your life in order for the government to keep control over you, to make sure you pay all your taxes and that you stay in line with their rules and regulations.
It is not you that allegedly owes the bank money; it is your legal fiction i.e. the company that you have been registered as that allegedly owes the money. How can you owe anything to anyone? You are simply a living spirit, a flesh and blood person, and if the government or banks claim that you owe them anything, how can they get it from you if you are not a registered part of the system? They cannot.

This is very confusing!

I know, but do not let this conversation be all that you do in order to understand what I am talking about. Go to Google, YouTube, or your local library. Buy some books and read what is happening in order for you to become an active part of the change that is about to occur. If you sit back and do nothing, the change will happen and you will be stuck in the same mindset that you live with today. The future needs critical thinking, ownership over responsibility and a collective consciousness that reaches out to create new ways of doing things so we can have a new way of experiencing life. Wouldn't you like to live in a world that allowed you to actually feel what it is to be free and not just hear about the possibility of freedom?

So if a company can only do business with a company does that mean that the tax man is a company and the government is a company?

Yes, the government of Ireland is a registered company and every single government department, as well as the departments within the departments are all individually registered companies including the court services of Ireland and each of the individual courts, the revenue services of Ireland, the health service, the police force (An Garda Siochana) and the list goes on as long as there is a public service doing business with the people of Ireland. All of their details are found online on the Dun and Bradstreet website where you will find their details and accounts.

So you are now essentially a company and that is the way the government can do business with you.

So I guess by having us signed over to the state as commodities we become security for the state, right?
Now you have it. Once you are signed in, your birth is monetised and you are used as collateral for borrowings. This is one of the real reasons behind the census.

What do you mean?
To monetise your birth cert means that the company that has just been formed is identified as a money making company for the government i.e. you. So in effect the government have a right to go to the banks they lend from and say 'look here, we have one million idiots, oh sorry, I mean people, who will work for forty or fifty years and give us a massive percentage of their earnings in what we are calling tax. This tax intake is equal to €x billion euro over the terms of their working life, can we borrow some money against this security please?' Of course the security is as good as gold so they borrow money against your registered name. This is known as monetisation. Do you see where this conversation has taken us?

Yes, right back to the institutions using us to generate money and make profit on the back of our blood, sweat and tears. However, if we were not registered we could not get a passport and we could not travel, is that right?

No that is incorrect but it is a great question. You have a right to travel in and out of the country you were born in even if you are not registered. There is a specific way to organise your passport in order to travel.

But if you have no registered name how can you sign a passport?
There is a specific way to do it, you need to investigate this yourself. Remember this conversation is not about giving you all the facts and details. It is about giving you enough information to create a driving force for you to do your home work. A good place to start in searching for more information on Google and YouTube is under the title 'Straw man'. Just follow the links and you will find everything you need.

But why don't you just tell me everything I need to know?
I am happy to point you in the right direction but I have found that unless people do their own research and get lost for a while in the overwhelming elements and aspects of this stuff they simply don't get it. It is the process of doing the research that allows you to really get it. Imagine you are learning to drive from a hand book and you are reading about driving for two years before sitting behind the wheel of a car, what do you think will happen the first time you turn on the ignition and try to drive the car? You know you will jump around for a bit before learning how to feel, hear or understand the car. You need to build the confidence to make certain

moves before you can feel that 'I've got it feeling'. It is from this feeling that you will experience a new level of confidence form which you will develop the skills to become a competent driver. It is the same with this stuff, learn it for yourself and watch your life change.

So does this mean that the Government can't just take tax from you?

Yes. However, I am not suggesting that we do not make a contribution to the ongoing development of the country but I am saying that the current system is flawed, dishonest and very unfair.

What is more, the Government understands what I am telling you but they will not tell you about it. However, in fairness to the government they don't take tax from you, tax is something that you agree to pay and they take with your agreement. If you are a PAYE worker you most certainly have a contract with your employer that you have signed giving them permission to take a certain amount of money from your wages in accordance with numbers provided by the government and if you are self employed then you voluntarily fill in and send off your paperwork every year with the taxes you believe you owe enclosed.

The most obvious way to see this in writing is to find someone that is self employed and look at the letter of receipt that is received from the revenue once they have made a payment. The letter will say something along the line of 'we have received your offer of €x and kindly agree to accept the same'. In doing this you are the one making the offer and they are simply accepting that offer.

But if you don't pay it they will take you to court, fine you and put you in jail if you continue to refuse to pay?
Yes, most likely

But if it a voluntary contribution how can they do that?

- Because you belong to them, remember you were signed over to their ownership as a child.
- Because you don't know enough about what being sovereign means.
- Because you live with assumptions and judgements in relation to what is right and wrong.
- Because they have the judge, the law and police on their side.
- Because nobody is going to challenge it.
- Because that is the way it has always been.
- Remember, I am not supporting the idea that we should not pay our way through life. However, I am saying that we need to understand that what is going on at the moment as IS NOT WORKING and begin to create a new way forward in order to offer people a chance to create a new quality of life.

But when did this sovereignty thing come about?
That question makes me laugh. That sovereignty thing has always been around. Sovereignty is something that

you are, you always have been and you always will be, but without understanding the true nature of life you are simply not going to understand it enough in order to allow the sovereign experience into your daily experience. Again, do the research. Make your life a journey of self-discovery because you will be amazed at what you find out about who you really are. If you look back at how the people of Ireland lived in Brehon Law times you will understand a lot more. There is a little more investigating for you to do. Before the English illegally occupied Ireland and enforced its rule on the land and the people of the country, Ireland had its own system of indigenous law that was more than progressive. In learning about your ancestors and lineage you will see things that you may never have imagined existed in Ireland. At one stage and for quite some time Ireland was a free country and the people managed very well without the systems that control and demand our lives from us today.

Are you suggesting that we go back in time?
I am not suggesting any such thing, I am however saying that life can be lived differently, but in order to create the change we must understand what we want to create, and in the process of we need to understand who we are, where we came from and what is possible.

It is a sad truth but for much of the history of this amazing land the people have been oppressed. There are stories buried within us that tell us that we are peasants, worthless, meaningless and powerless and it is these stories that are informing us today. They are in our DNA, which is part of the reason why nobody has taken to the streets and demanded that we find a way out of the euro and the European game of financial control. We are still living from a consciousness of oppression and worthlessness. We are infected with the curse of catholic guilt and the fear of what people will think of us if we stick our heads above the parapet. But remember that this life is a gift we are creating in order to evolve and grow into the best version of who we are. Sitting back and allowing life to be controlled by the institutionalised systems is simply going to create a future driven by more oppression. It is time to agree as a community that we are not going to remain focused on the things that take from us, and instead tune into a heart and mind of love, compassion, support and creation. I will say it again, the future is in our hands, and it is the people of Ireland that will create the future whether we do something or do nothing. I would like to believe that we will do something.

So let me get this right, are you saying that the Government, the Law, the banks and the other systems we respond to only have power over us if we allow them to have this power?

Bingo! As they say in County Monaghan, 'now you're sucking diesel'. The only power someone has over you is the power you give them and the power you allow them to have over you is a direct reflection of the power you feel you do or do not have in your own life.

We have continually elected people into office in Ireland who have let us down by not prioritising the people. But these people have been looking outward to the world in order to build what is here. What they missed was that we can learn from the world but we need to stay grounded in who we are, what we can achieve and what we need in order to be happy and at peace. If you asked most people if they would rather be happy or wealthy most of them would say happy as we all know that money cannot buy that rare reality.

I say that we can be happy and wealthy but the wealth I refer to goes beyond material wealth. I mean the wealth of heart and mind and once we have that, the material wealth will follow, just as a man who is at peace can find within himself the stuff of miracles and a nation joined together with a vision, a community experience, trust, love, peace and respect for each one as if it were their own kin will create their dream too.

Tell me more about the sovereignty, I'm excited about that...

Once you live in the consciousness of sovereignty life becomes a whole new experience. It gets easier and more meaningful as you begin to learn about and experience your true nature. There is nothing that has a command over you other than your own sense of self and that sense of self is informed by how you life and how the community around you treat you. The sovereign person lives to help others, to fulfil his purpose, to learn what is need to die in peace and not to resist that moment of leaving here to go to wherever he believes he must go. The sovereign person knows that he is free and he lives

accordingly by giving what he has to those who need it and trusting that he will be given all that he needs.
Even the constitution of Ireland recognises the sovereignty of the person when it refers to the fact that no law stands above man other than the law of God. What you can learn from this is that the constitution of your country claims that even the legal courts have no power over he who knows he is sovereign.

When you talk about God are you talking about religion?
No, this has nothing to do with religion nor has God. God is the source of all things, the order in the chaos, the meaning in the meaningless. You can call God by the name 'life' or 'spirit' or just find a word that works for you but be sure to know that God and religion are not necessarily connected and have little connection at all, if any. Religion is just another institution, another business and illusion that is filled with manmade rules that are designed to control freedom. Of course, that is just my opinion which I do not claim that to be the truth for anyone else.

How can you let the Government know that you are sovereign and not willing to play their game anymore?
Pretty soon you won't have to tell them. Life is doing what is needed to bring the systems into a clear understanding of that reality. Just a little more time and you will see the sovereign understanding of life take it

rightful place in the minds and hearts of the people of this great country. I know that life is very tough for many people at the moment but what is coming down the road is a whole new experience, understanding and a fantastic rising of the true nature of who we are.

Patrick & Lisa

Patrick & Lisa are both in the early fifties, they always kept a perfect credit rating with their banks and made it their business to ensure that monthly bills were paid on time. They never experienced difficulty with the bank, nor the bank with them. However, that all changed in 2010. Patrick approached the bank for a small overdraft of €7,000 for some maintenance work that was required on a number of his properties that he had accumulated as part of his property plan. The bank refused and explained that he would need to pay for the maintenance out of his businesses cash flow. He responded that the business was in good condition and his record with the bank was exceptional. Still, the bank refused. Not only that but they also informed him that they would have to review his loan arrangements as they were tracker based and they wanted him to change to a more favourable agreement (for the bank of course). Eventually the bank agreed to offer him a €1,000 overdraft on the condition that a valuation was done on the properties. Patrick felt it worthless to pay €400 for a valuation simply to qualify for a €1,000 overdraft so he declined the offer.
This situation left both Patrick and Lisa confused. They clearly felt aggrieved that after maintaining a perfect credit rating, the bank would close the door on them.

At this stage Patrick began to reach into his knowledge base and pull forward some information that he had learned over the years but hadn't really given much attention to. He had heard a lot about how the banks work, in terms of clients being pawns in their game. He never thought there was much to this information but now he was curious and he began to investigate the world of finance and banking. After some time of study Patrick was clear that something was not right in relation to how the banks were doing business.

His studies brought him to a place of understanding that there should be a contract in place in order for a loan to be legal and lawful. He found it strange that the bank had never invoiced him for any payments and he also discovered that if the bank were truly harmed and injured by a person not repaying a loan they should be able to show the loss in their books and this would act as proof that the money and loan truly existed and the debt must be repaid. He also learned about the securitization process, what it means in terms of the bank selling off his loan to another party (or a number of parties) and the truth about money being an illusion.

Patrick and Lisa decided to write to the bank and request proof that the business they were engaged in with the bank was legal and lawful and both the money and the loan were in fact real and not simply illusionary. In the mean time they made a decision to withhold payments until they received the proof they were requesting as they felt they did not want to continue paying into a system of fraud and swindling.

The first letter they wrote was a simple request for proof of the legal and lawful standing of the alleged debt by requesting a copy of the contract, an invoice and/or validation of the debt by the bank showing the loss that existed in their books as a result of this loan not being repaid. The following is a copy of the letter sent:

Letter One sent by Patrick & Lisa

Mr.

July 2011

Re: Account Number:

Dear Mr. Murphy,

We wrote to you on of July last, requesting the following documentation, so that we may settle any financial obligation we might lawfully owe:

1. Validation of the debt (the actual accounting);

2. Verification of your claim against us (a sworn affidavit or a hand signed invoice in accordance with Bills of Exchange Act (1882));

3. A copy of the contract signed by both parties and therefore binding both parties.

As you have failed to provide the aforementioned documentation to validate your claim, we hereby give you ten (10) days to reply to this notice from the above date with a notice sent using recorded post and signed under full commercial liability and penalties of perjury, assuring and promising us that all of the replies and details given to the above requests are true and without deception, fraud or mischief. Your said failure to provide the aforementioned documentation within ten (10) days, from the above date, to validate the debt, will constitute your agreement to the following terms:

1. That the debt did not exist in the first place.
OR
2. It has already been paid in full.
AND

No assured value, No liability. Errors & Omissions Excepted. All Rights Reserved. 1
WITHOUT PREJUDICE – WITHOUT RECOURSE – NON-ASSUMPSIT

This is not a complaint or a query or a request for a statement, agreement, offer letter or terms and conditions, and is not to be treated as one.

Please Note: We wish to deal with this matter in writing and we do not give your organisation permission to contact us by telephone. We ask that you respect our legal rights and reputation and refrain from involving any third parties in this matter.

We look forward to hearing from you.

Sincerely Yours in Honour and Respect

By:

By: Sovereign [redacted] Authorised Representative

The bank refused to send the information as requested and they simply forwarded a copy of a loan agreement, a copy of bank statements and a copy of the other incidental documentation that they had on file. Patrick and Lisa wrote once again requesting the exact information that they had asked for in their first letter.

They were aware that an agreement was not a contract and they were now anxious to see the official documentation that existed within the bank that proved beyond reasonable doubt that they owed the bank money.

Their thinking was very simple, Patrick claimed 'surely if the bank has proof they will produce it and if they do that will solve the problem and we along with our letters will soon stop annoying the bank'.

The next letter was sent in order to remind the bank that they had made a request for specific information and that information was not received. This letter made the same request and once again Patrick & Lisa gave the bank 10 days to respond.

Patrick was learning much about the legal system and his rights in terms of requesting information, what information to request and who to request it from.

Along the way Patrick had sought much support from solicitors and other professionals within the legal system but to no avail; he was simply informed that he should stop requesting the information as he was and simply pay the banks. His attempts to understand this brought nothing only further frustration, he couldn't understand why the legal fraternity were supporting the banks that clearly could not provide, or were refusing to provide the documentation that he believed would show the banking world as nothing other than a game that was now taking from the people all they had worked for.

Letter Two sent by Patrick & Lisa

Mr.

July 2011

Re: Account Number:

Dear Mr. Murphy,

We wrote to you on of July last, requesting the following documentation, so that we may settle any financial obligation we might lawfully owe:

1. Validation of the debt (the actual accounting);

2. Verification of your claim against us (a sworn affidavit or a hand signed invoice in accordance with Bills of Exchange Act (1882));

3. A copy of the contract signed by both parties and therefore binding both parties.

As you have failed to provide the aforementioned documentation to validate your claim, we hereby give you ten (10) days to reply to this notice from the above date with a notice sent using recorded post and signed under full commercial liability and penalties of perjury, assuring and promising us that all of the replies and details given to the above requests are true and without deception, fraud or mischief. Your said failure to provide the aforementioned documentation within ten (10) days, from the above date, to validate the debt, will constitute your agreement to the following terms:

1. That the debt did not exist in the first place.
OR
2. It has already been paid in full.
AND

3. That any damages we suffer, you will be held culpable.
4. That any negative remarks made to a credit reference agency will be removed.
5. You will no longer pursue this matter any further.
6. You agree to pay all fee schedules.

Furthermore, we will not enter into any verbal communication over the telephone. We will only accept written responses for our records. *We ask that you respect our legal rights and refrain from involving any third parties.*

Sincerely Yours in Honour and Respect

By:

By: Sovereign [redacted] Authorised Representative

No assured value, No liability. Errors & Omissions Excepted. All Rights Reserved. 2
WITHOUT PREJUDICE – WITHOUT RECOURSE – NON-ASSUMPSIT

Patrick sent a further letter letting the bank know that he was not at all happy with the fact they continually refused to forward the documentation as requested. At this stage he was sure as a result of his investigations and studies that the bank were involved in fraud, engaged in misrepresentation and were lying to him about the true nature of his relationship with them, with him and the true nature of the business they were engaged in. His third letter stated very clearly that he wanted answers to his questions and he was not resting until this was dealt with.

Letter Three sent by Patrick & Lisa

Mr.

August 2011

Account Notice of suspension of this account pending supply of documentation within 10 days to disprove FRAUD

Dear Mr. Murphy,

Subsequent to our letters dated of July 2011 and the of July 2011 we are now in receipt of further information leading us to believe that apart from there not being any valid contract or agreement in existence, the practice you have been engaged in makes any contract entered into void, as it was incepted in fraud.

If an issue of fraud or misrepresentation is demonstrated at the inception of a contract then the contract itself becomes unreliable and has no force. Furthermore all subsections of any agreement including those of passing personal information to third party collectors or collection agencies also become null and void as the total agreement or application was conceived in fraud.

Specifically it is now apparent that you have been engaged in transactions and activities (covered amongst others under the **Bills of Exchange Act 1882**) and have:

1. Converted the initial supposed agreement or document into a **Bill of Exchange** or **Promissory Note** without our knowledge or consent, thus rendering any agreement invalid at its inception due to non-disclosure and gross misrepresentation.

2. Created money on this basis without our knowledge or consent.

3. Used this money as an agent without our authority.

4. Taken commission on this money by selling this instrument funding to the merchant, the merchants bank without our knowledge or consent.

5. Mislead us to believe we or the above party were receiving a loan or credit line from you separately and validly obtained variable assets, where in fact there were no such assets and thus no loan or credit.

6. Charged interest on this supposed loan or credit when in fact there was none supplied.

No assured value, No liability. Errors & Omissions Excepted. All Rights Reserved.
WITHOUT PREJUDICE – WITHOUT RECOURSE – NON-ASSUMPSIT

The above actions constitute fraudulent activity and we demand nullification of the entire contract as we firmly believe fraud has taken place.

We hereby kindly request the three items of evidence below by recorded delivery under 1-3 below along with a cover letter with comment replying to each point numbered as below. Failure to provide the above evidence within ten (10) days of the date of this presentment will deem your claims irrelevant and that the undersigned reserves every right to have effected settlement and closure in the private.

1) Certified Copy of Contract Documentation signed by both parties (including both sides of the application form).
With respect to this, we wish to note that to satisfy a lawfully valid contract, the contract needs to have:
A) Full Disclosure

It appears that while ostensibly making a loan or credit facility to the above named/numbered account, you have not in fact lent any money against any actual funds (i.e. assets such as the banks or other depositors' deposits). This is required to comply with (amongst others) the Banking Law and International GAAP rules (Generally Accepted Accounting Principles) and or the UK ASB (Accounting Standards Board).

We gather that in fact you actually made bookkeeping entries, artificially 'creating' an asset in your books based on converting our application form into a promissory note and this without our knowledge or consent. Furthermore, even though there has been an exchange of value for value, you are then 'lending' against this asset of 'ours' that you have created, and then charging interest on a 'loan' or 'credit facility ' you have never in fact made.

Unless you can demonstrate otherwise, does this not constitute a lack of full disclosure? If you did not actually appropriately lend any money, would any original supposed contract not be rendered null and void?

B) Equal Consideration

In a contract, both parties must provide consideration. If no real loan or credit line facility is actually provided then you have not provided any consideration. If this is the case, is it not true that you have no possibility of any loss?

C) Lawful Terms and Conditions

Please advise how – if money has been created based on the conversion of our application form into a 'promissory note', this satisfies the requirement of a lawful contract.

D) Signed by both parties

A valid contract must be evidenced, signed and dated by both parties. Please detail explicitly who has signed for yourselves, what position they hold and where the signature is evidenced.

For the avoidance of doubt a copy of the Terms and Conditions does NOT satisfy our above request. Also we are formally requesting that any certified copy is accompanied by a cover letter describing how the documents meet all the above criteria A) to C).

2) Validation of any debt we may owe.

Please kindly supply:

a) Copies of evidence of the proper accounting as to the source of the actual funds being loaned (i.e. at the inception of the account).

b) Details of whose assets actually funded the credit facility and how;

c) Evidence as to whether the funding was in place before our application was received or whether our application created the "credit" or "loan" facility.

NB: Please note carefully that "statements" showing subsequent transactions do not satisfy or verify this requirement and are not what we are asking for. Neither is this a US or UK only requirement. This is standard commercial Irish law practice. If you intend to state this is not the case please provide a sworn affidavit under your full personal and commercial liability of how this is not applicable to Irish law and legislation.

3) Verification of any claim against us

Please supply as above i.e. a signed invoice or sworn affidavit stating what money you have lent to which named party.

If you intend to state this is not required, we would advise that this is required under Irish law for example under the standard courts procedure including the Discovery Rules and notice to Procedure Documents. If you intend to state this is not the case please provide a sworn affidavit under your full personal and commercial liability of how this is not applicable to Irish law.

Any statement without this will not be accepted as it has no standing.

4) Credit Reference Agencies

If you are not able to provide us with the above stated three items, then we are herewith also formally asking for written confirmation that any records that you have forwarded to any credit reference agency are removed from any credit file held by them, as there will not be any evidence of debt (or non-payment of same) to support any credit record, adverse or otherwise.

May we bring to your attention the following: " **Any activity on this alleged claim while it is in question is also a violation of related consumer protection acts, and may also be in violation of Irish laws".**

5) EU Directives – Unfair Commercial Practices Directives

Under the EU Unfair Commercial Practices Directive (Misleading Practices and Omissions); A commercial practice is *misleading* if it either:

- Contains false information and is therefore untruthful, or
- In any way, including overall presentation, deceives or is likely to deceive *the average*

No assured value, No liability. Errors & Omissions Excepted. All Rights Reserved.
WITHOUT PREJUDICE – WITHOUT RECOURSE – NON-ASSUMPSIT

consumer; even if the information is correct and,
- Causes or is likely to cause him to take a transactional decision that he would have otherwise not taken.

The criteria are objective, so there is no need to prove that a consumer was actually misled. The possibility of deception alone can be considered misleading, if the other elements are present as well. There is no need to prove a financial loss.

Omissions refer to the fact that consumers need information to make informed choices. A trader must provide material information that the average consumer needs. It is misleading to:

- Omit material information that the average consumer needs, according to the context, to take an informed transactional decision;
- Hide or provide material information in an unclear, unintelligible, ambiguous or untimely manner;
- Fail to identify the commercial intent of the commercial practice if not already apparent from the context.

When assessing practices for omissions, the following aspects are taken into consideration:

- What counts is the effect of the commercial practice in its entirety, including the presentation; information must be displayed clearly; obscure presentation is tantamount to an omission to inform.

There has been a clear and obvious failure to investigate and provide details as appropriate in this matter. If you are unable to provide the above three documents, please be kind enough to advise how this does not constitute a breach of these EU directives.

6) Third Parties

Third parties, such as solicitors or debt collection agents or agencies, do not – as third parties – have any jurisdiction in any matter between the above titled party and yourselves. We also explicitly state herewith that we do not give any permission for you to pass on any personal details relating to the above account to such agencies and explicitly revoke any actual or implied permission previously granted. Should the original contract be valid, then this revocation stands by novation if not rebutted.

7) Communication

Please make all communication with respect to this issue in writing only by recorded delivery and confirm you will comply and not contact us by phone or allow anyone else to contact us by phone or email.

Required by law under the Bills of Exchange Act 1882 you have 3 days to respond, however we are agreeable to allow you and your company 10 days to supply the requested information. Kindly refer to each above numbered item 1 through 7 specifically in your reply.

Unless you, **Bank of Ireland**, can furnish to us proof of claim and signed affidavit, within the next ten (10) days of the date of this letter, it shall be taken as your lawful admission the debt has been discharged / extinguished under the accepted and appropriate terms regarding primary liability of

No assured value, No liability. Errors & Omissions Excepted. All Rights Reserved.
WITHOUT PREJUDICE – WITHOUT RECOURSE – NON-ASSUMPSIT

instruments, and the account is settled and closed. You also will admit and agree that:

That we are the depositor(s) for this account, that **Bank of Ireland** risked none of **Bank of Ireland** assets at any time regarding this account and that **Bank of Ireland** failed to disclose these facts to us.

Take notice we hold you personally accountable under your full commercial liability, for any personal financial or other damages incurred as a result of any action proceeding **Bank of Ireland** or any of its employees or agents, in the absence of any proof of claim, signed affidavit, and supporting documentation.

A fee schedule / service charge list will be presented to you and applied should you proceed with any action without first presenting facts and an opportunity to cure, and we also advise you that if the information is not forthcoming, it will be reported to the Court that you are trying to frustrate proceedings and denying us the opportunity to file a defence and counter claim.

With conditional acceptance in mind, we write to you today and in doing so we state that we will be happy to settle any financial obligation that we might lawfully owe when we receive the three documents listed below:

1. **Validation of the debt – The actual accounting**
2. **Verification of your claim against us, i.e. A sworn affidavit or Signed invoice**
3. **A copy of the contract binding both parties**

You have ten (10) days to comply with our request.

Sincerely Yours in Honour and Respect

By:

By: Sovereign [redacted] Authorised Representative

No assured value, No liability. Errors & Omissions Excepted. All Rights Reserved.
WITHOUT PREJUDICE – WITHOUT RECOURSE – NON-ASSUMPSIT

The following is a copy of the final letter Patrick sent:

Mr.

Date: of August 2011

Private & Confidential

Notice to Agent is Notice to Principal
Notice to Principal is Notice to Agent

The undersigned is I as I is the undersigned

Acceptance of Claim for Settlement and Closure

Dear Mr. Murphy,

We wish to meet our lawful obligations and this is not a refusal to pay, nor has there been or will be any refusal to pay.

Subsequent to our letters dated of July, of July, and the of August last, we have recently been informed that **Bank of Ireland Ltd account** date unknown, may contain fraud and is unlawful.

We conditionally accept your claim (if any) for purported outstanding balance upon proof of claim and under your full commercial liability that the facts are true, complete, certain and not misleading, with your insurance number and insurance provider details, that:

1. Proof of Claim that you furnish the original legal document (or a copy independently certified by a third party – a copy of front and rear sides of each page) that evidences the signed contract between **Bank of Ireland Ltd** and

2. Proof of Claim that Irish or Euro legal tender isn't fiat currency and that there is money/currency of substance in common circulation in Ireland with which to extinguish the debt.

3. Proof of Claim that demanding payment with Euro currency/money in order to 'pay' a purported debt would be discharging the debt not augmenting the debt.

4. Proof of Claim that we are the 'person's' or entity and not the Sovereign Living Breathing Life Force of Men and Women, of the family

No assured value, No liability. Errors & Omissions Excepted. All Rights Reserved.
WITHOUT PREJUDICE – WITHOUT RECOURSE – NON-ASSUMPSIT

5. Proof of Claim that **Bank of Ireland Ltd** has sustained a loss, verified by a valid signed invoice sworn under their full commercial liability by a bona fide representative of **Bank of Ireland Ltd** who has the power to bind the both parties in contract.

6. Proof of Claim that a contract that contains any element of fraud/deception is not null and void.

7. Proof of Claim that to discharge the purported debt, **Bank of Ireland Ltd** could not furnish a Bill of Exchange or like instrument to undersigned for his signature in order to discharge the purported debt.

If any provision of this agreement is found not to be enforceable in a court of competent jurisdiction, it shall not adversely affect any other provision of this agreement and reasonable opportunity and effect shall be taken to modify it to become enforceable.

Failure to provide the above evidence within ten (10) days of the date of this presentment will deem your claims irrelevant and that the undersigned reserves every right to have effected settlement and closure in the private.

Unless you / **Bank of Ireland Ltd** can furnish us a proof of claim and signed affidavit, within the next **ten (10)** days of the date of this presentment, including mailing, it is taken as your lawful admission the debt has been discharged / extinguished under the accepted and appropriate terms regarding primary liability of instruments, and the account is settled and closed. You also will admit and agree that:

1. To report this account to all credit bureaus as ' paid as agreed'

2. That we are the depositor's for this account, that **Bank of Ireland Ltd** risked none of **Bank of Ireland Ltd** assets at any time regarding this account and that **Bank of Ireland Ltd** failed to disclose these facts to us.

3. The date of the last activity on this account is the date of this notice

Take Notice we hold **you** personally accountable under your full commercial liability, for any personal financial or other damages incurred as a result of any or all action proceedings **Bank of Ireland Ltd** or any of its employees or agents, in the absence of any proof of claim, signed affidavit, and supporting documentation. A fee schedule / service charge list will be presented to you and applied should you proceed with any action without first presenting facts and an opportunity to cure and we also advise you that if the information is not forthcoming, it will be reported to the court that you are trying to frustrate proceedings and denying us the opportunity to file a defence and counter claim.

Furthermore, we will not enter into any verbal communication over the phone. We will only accept written responses delivered by recorded mail for our records. *We respectfully request that you respect our legal rights and reputation and refrain from involving any third parties to this civil matter.*

No assured value, No liability. Errors & Omissions Excepted. All Rights Reserved.
WITHOUT PREJUDICE – WITHOUT RECOURSE – NON-ASSUMPSIT

You have ten (10) days to comply.

Sincerely Yours in Honour and Respect

By:

By: Sovereign [redacted] uthorised Representative

No assured value, No liability. Errors & Omissions Excepted. All Rights Reserved.
WITHOUT PREJUDICE – WITHOUT RECOURSE – NON-ASSUMPSIT

Patrick and Lisa are a perfect example of two people who took the situation with the bank seriously and they began to investigate what had happened and why. They were determined to highlight the fraud they were now aware the banks were involved in. In fact, the further they investigated the banking world and the nature of money the more they realised the true extent of the game and the clearer it became to them that the banks were creating, supporting and covering up the greatest con of all times.

The bank has continually refused to provide the paperwork that Patrick & Lisa have requested and they are now threatening court action in order to repossess the properties in question.

This is a typical example of what is happening throughout Ireland, people are asking questions and being ignored. People are seeking help and being left alone, looking for information and being kept in the dark and trusting a system that is designed to take from them. They don't know where to go, what to do or understand how to deal with their situation, and the government is continuing to sell them, their homes, their life savings, their futures, their children's future and their hopes to Europe. FOR WHAT? Are the people of Ireland not the primary concern of the Government of Ireland?

Together we can make the change happen. It is time to speak up or live in the pain.